180 Days of SCIENCE
for Fifth Grade

Author
Lauren Homayoun

SHELL EDUCATION

Earth & Space
Life
Physical

Publishing Credits

Corinne Burton, M.A.Ed., *Publisher*
Conni Medina, M.A.Ed., *Managing Editor*
Emily R. Smith, M.A.Ed., *Content Director*
Shaun Bernadou, *Art Director*
Lynette Ordoñez, *Editor*

Image Credits

P.91 Keith Homan/Shutterstock.com; p.159 jukurae/Shutterstock.com;
all other images from iStock and/or Shutterstock.

Standards

© 2014 Mid-continent Research for Education and Learning (McREL)
NGSS Lead States. 2013. Next Generation Science Standards: For States, By States.
Washington, DC: The National Academies Press.

For information on how this resource meets national and other state standards, see pages 10–13. You may also review this information by visiting our website at www.teachercreatedmaterials.com/administrators/correlations/ and following the on-screen directions.

Shell Education

A division of Teacher Created Materials
5301 Oceanus Drive
Huntington Beach, CA 92649-1030
www.tcmpub.com/shell-education

ISBN 978-1-4258-1411-3
©2018 Shell Educational Publishing, Inc.

Table of Contents

Introduction

With today's science and technology, there are more resources than ever to help students understand how the world works. Information about science experiments you can do at home is widely available online. Many students have experience with physics concepts from games.

While students may be familiar with many of the topics discussed in this book, it is not uncommon for them to have misconceptions about certain subjects. It is important for students to learn how to apply scientific practices in a classroom setting and within their lives.

Science is the study of the physical and natural world through observation and experiment. Not only is it important for students to learn scientific facts, but it is important for them to develop a thirst for knowledge. This leads to students who are anxious to learn and who understand how to follow practices that will lead them to the answers they seek.

The Need for Practice

To be successful in science, students must understand how people interact with the physical world. They must not only master scientific practices but also learn how to look at the world with curiosity. Through repeated practice, students will learn how a variety of factors affect the world in which they live.

Understanding Assessment

In addition to providing opportunities for frequent practice, teachers must be able to assess students' scientific understandings. This allows teachers to adequately address students' misconceptions, build on their current understandings, and challenge them appropriately. Assessment is a long-term process that involves careful analysis of student responses from discussions, projects, or practice sheets. The data gathered from assessments should be used to inform instruction: slow down, speed up, or reteach. This type of assessment is called *formative assessment*.

How to Use This Book

Weekly Structure

All 36 weeks of this book follow a regular weekly structure. The book is divided into three sections: Life Science, Physical Science, and Earth and Space Science. The book is structured to give students a strong foundation on which to build throughout the year. It is also designed to adequately prepare them for state standardized tests.

Each week focuses on one topic. Day 1 sets the stage by providing background information on the topic that students will need throughout the week. In Day 2, students analyze data related to the topic. Day 3 leads students through developing scientific questions. Day 4 guides students through planning a solution. Finally, Day 5 helps students communicate results from observations or investigations.

 Day 1—Learning Content: Students will read grade-appropriate content and answer questions about it.

 Day 2—Analyzing Data: Students will analyze scientific data and answer questions about it.

 Day 3—Developing Questions: Students will read a scenario related to the topic, answer questions, and formulate a scientific question about the information.

 Day 4—Planning Solutions: Students will read a scenario related to the topic, answer questions, and develop a solution or plan an investigation.

 Day 5—Communicating Results: Students accurately communicate the results of an investigation or demonstrate what they learned throughout the week.

Three Strands of Science

This book allows students to explore the three strands of science: life science, physical science, and earth and space science. Life science teaches students about the amazing living things on our planet and how they interact in ecosystems. Physical science introduces students to physics and chemistry concepts that will lay the groundwork for deeper understanding later in their education. Earth and space science familiarizes students with the wonders of the cosmos and the relationships between the sun, Earth, moon, and stars.

How to Use This Book *(cont.)*

Weekly Topics

The following chart shows the weekly focus topics that are covered during each week of instruction.

Unit	Week	Science Topic
Life Science	1	Life Cycles
	2	The Life Cycle of Humans
	3	The Life Cycle of Reptiles
	4	Vertebrates and Invertebrates
	5	Human Traits
	6	Animal Traits
	7	Food Chains
	8	Food Chains in the Jungle
	9	Plant Needs
	10	The Role of Decomposers
	11	How Plants Create Food
	12	Ecosystems
Physical Science	1	Can Matter Disappear?
	2	How Do We Know Air is There?
	3	How Air Moves Things
	4	When Combining Matter, Mass Stays the Same
	5	Mass Stays the Same When Water Changes States
	6	Identifying Powers and Minerals
	7	Properties of Metals
	8	Creating New Substances–Physical and Chemical Changes
	9	Understanding Physical and Chemical Changes
	10	How Energy from the Sun Feeds Us
	11	How Energy Flows through Food Chains
	12	Gravity
Earth and Space Science	1	Oceans and Ecosystems
	2	Winds and Clouds in Mountain Ranges
	3	Fresh Water in Rivers and Lakes
	4	The Polar Ice Caps
	5	Agriculture, Industry, and the Environment
	6	Protecting Our Water Sources
	7	Earth's Orbit
	8	Day and Night on Earth
	9	Is the Sun Our Brightest Star?
	10	The Motion of the Stars
	11	Constellations Visible During Different Seasons
	12	The Movement of Shadows

How to Use This Book *(cont.)*

Best Practices for This Series

- Use the practice pages to introduce important science topics to your students.

- Use the Weekly Topics chart on page 5 to align the content to what you're covering in class. Then, treat the pages in this book as jumping off points for that content.

- Use the practice pages as formative assessment of the science strands and key topics.

- Use the weekly themes to engage students in content that is new to them.

- Encourage students to independently learn more about the topics introduced in this series.

- Lead teacher-directed discussions of the vocabulary and concepts presented in some of the more complex weeks.

- Support students in practicing the varied types of questions asked throughout the practice pages.

- When possible, have students participate in hands-on activities to answer the questions they generate and do the investigations they plan.

Using the Resources

An answer key for all days can be found on pages 194–206. Rubrics for Day 3 (developing questions), Day 4 (planning solutions), and Day 5 (communicating results) can be found on pages 210–212 and in the Digital Resources. Use the answer keys and rubrics to assess students' work. Be sure to share these rubrics with students so that they know what is expected of them.

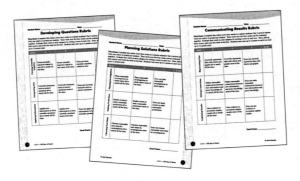

How to Use This Book *(cont.)*

Diagnostic Assessment

Teachers can use the practice pages as diagnostic assessments. The data analysis tools included with the book enable teachers or parents to quickly score students' work and monitor their progress. Teachers and parents can see which skills students may need to target further to develop proficiency.

Students will learn science content, how to analyze data, how to develop scientific questions, how to plan solutions, and how to accurately communicate results. You can assess students' learning using the answer key for all days. Rubrics are also provided on pages 210–212 for Days 3–5 to help you further assess key analytical skills that are needed for success with the scientific practices. Then, record their scores on the Practice Page Item Analysis sheets (pages 213–215). These charts are provided as PDFs, Microsoft Word® files, and Microsoft Excel® files. Teachers can input data into the electronic files directly, or they can print the pages.

To Complete the Practice Page Analysis Charts

- Write or type students' names in the far-left column. Depending on the number of students, more than one copy of the form may be needed or you may need to add rows.

  - The science strands are indicated across the tops of the charts.

  - Students should be assessed every four weeks, as indicated in the first rows of the charts.

- For each student, evaluate his or her work over the past four weeks using the answer key for Days 1 and 2 and the rubrics for Days 3–5.

- Review students' work for the weeks indicated in the chart. For example, if using the *Life Science Analysis Chart* for the first time, review students' work from weeks 1–4. Add the scores for Days 1 and 2 for each student, and record those in the appropriate columns. Then, write students' rubric scores for Days 3–5 in the corresponding columns. Use these scores as benchmarks to determine how each student is performing.

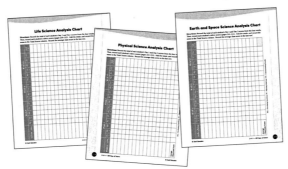

Digital Resources

The Digital Resources contain digital copies of the rubrics, analysis sheets, and standards correlations. See page 216 for more information.

How to Use This Book *(cont.)*

Using the Results to Differentiate Instruction

Once results are gathered and analyzed, teachers can use the results to inform the way they differentiate instruction. The data can help determine which science skills and topics are the most difficult for students and which students need additional instructional support and continued practice.

Whole-Class Support

The results of the diagnostic analysis may show that the entire class is struggling with certain science topics. If these concepts have been taught in the past, this indicates that further instruction or reteaching is necessary. If these concepts have not been taught in the past, this data is a great preassessment and may demonstrate that students do not have a working knowledge of the concepts. Thus, careful planning for the length of the unit(s) or lesson(s) must be considered, and additional front-loading may be required.

Small-Group or Individual Support

The results of the diagnostic analysis may show that an individual student or a small group of students is struggling with certain science skills. If these concepts have been taught in the past, this indicates that further instruction or reteaching is necessary. Consider pulling these students aside to instruct them further on the concepts while others are working independently. Students may also benefit from extra practice using games or computer-based resources.

Teachers can also use the results to help identify proficient individual students or groups of students who are ready for enrichment or above-grade-level instruction. These students may benefit from independent learning contracts or more challenging activities.

Standards Correlations

Shell Education is committed to producing educational materials that are research and standards based. In this effort, we have correlated all of our products to the academic standards of all 50 states, the District of Columbia, the Department of Defense Dependents Schools, and all Canadian provinces.

How to Find Standards Correlations

To print a customized correlation report of this product for your state, visit our website at **www.teachercreatedmaterials.com/administrators/correlations/** and follow the on-screen directions. If you require assistance in printing correlation reports, please contact our Customer Service Department at 1-877-777-3450.

Purpose and Intent of Standards

The Every Student Succeeds Act (ESSA) mandates that all states adopt challenging academic standards that help students meet the goal of college and career readiness. While many states already adopted academic standards prior to ESSA, the act continues to hold states accountable for detailed and comprehensive standards.

Standards are designed to focus instruction and guide adoption of curricula. Standards are statements that describe the criteria necessary for students to meet specific academic goals. They define the knowledge, skills, and content students should acquire at each level. Standards are also used to develop standardized tests to evaluate students' academic progress. Teachers are required to demonstrate how their lessons meet state standards. State standards are used in the development of all of our products, so educators can be assured they meet the academic requirements of each state.

McREL Compendium

Each year, McREL analyzes state standards and revises the compendium to produce a general compilation of national standards. The standards listed on page 10 support the objectives presented throughout the weeks.

Next Generation Science Standards

This set of national standards aims to incorporate knowledge and process standards into a cohesive framework. The standards listed on pages 10–13 support the objectives presented throughout the weeks.

Standards Correlations *(cont.)*

180 Days of Science is designed to give students daily practice in the three strands of science. The weeks support the McREL standards and NGSS performance expectations listed in the charts below.

McREL Standards		
Standard	**Weeks**	**Unit**
Knows that plants and animals progress through life cycles of birth, growth and development, reproduction, and death; the details of these life cycles are different for different organisms.	1, 2	Life Science
Knows different ways in which living things can be grouped and purposes of different groupings.	3, 4	Life Science
Knows that many characteristics of plants and animals are inherited from its parents, and other characteristics result from an individual's interactions with the environment.	5, 6	Life Science
Knows the organization of simple food chains and food webs.	7, 8	Life Science
Knows that materials may be composed of parts that are too small to be seen without magnification.	1–3	Physical Science
Knows that substances can be classified by their physical and chemical properties.	6, 7	Physical Science
Knows that the Earth's gravity pulls any object toward it without touching it.	12	Physical Science
Knows how features on the Earth's surface are constantly changed by a combination of slow and rapid processes.	1, 2	Earth and Space Science
Knows that the Earth is one of several planets that orbit the Sun and that the Moon orbits the Earth.	7	Earth and Space Science
Knows that night and day are caused by the Earth's rotation on its axis.	8	Earth and Space Science
Knows that astronomical objects in space are massive in size and are separated from one another by vast distances.	9	Earth and Space Science
Knows that the patterns of stars in the sky stay the same, although they appear to slowly move from east to west across the sky nightly and different stars can be seen in different seasons.	10, 12	Earth and Space Science

Next Generation Science Standards					
Unit	**Week**	**Performance Expectation**	**Science and Engineering Practices**	**Disciplinary Core Ideas**	**Cross-Cutting Concepts**
Life Science	1	Develop a model to describe the movement of matter among plants, animals, decomposers, and the environment.	Science Models, Laws, Mechanisms, and Theories Explain Natural Phenomena	N/A	Systems and System Models
	2	Develop a model to describe the movement of matter among plants, animals, decomposers, and the environment.	Science Models, Laws, Mechanisms, and Theories Explain Natural Phenomena	N/A	Systems and System Models
	3	Develop a model to describe the movement of matter among plants, animals, decomposers, and the environment.	Developing and Using Models	N/A	Systems and System Models

Standards Correlations *(cont.)*

Unit	Week	Performance Expectation	Science and Engineering Practices	Disciplinary Core Ideas	Cross-Cutting Concepts
		Next Generation Science Standards			
Life Science	4	Develop a model to describe the movement of matter among plants, animals, decomposers, and the environment.	Developing and Using Models	N/A	Systems and System Models
	5	Develop a model to describe the movement of matter among plants, animals, decomposers, and the environment.	Science Models, Laws, Mechanisms, and Theories Explain Natural Phenomena	N/A	Systems and System Models
	6	Develop a model to describe the movement of matter among plants, animals, decomposers, and the environment.	Science Models, Laws, Mechanisms, and Theories Explain Natural Phenomena	N/A	Systems and System Models
	7	Develop a model to describe the movement of matter among plants, animals, decomposers, and the environment.	Developing and Using Models	Organization for Matter and Energy Flow in Organisms	Systems and System Models; Energy and Matter
	8	Develop a model to describe the movement of matter among plants, animals, decomposers, and the environment.	Developing and Using Models	Organization for Matter and Energy Flow in Organisms	Systems and System Models; Energy and Matter
	9	Support an argument that plants get the materials they need for growth chiefly from air and water.	Engaging in Argument from Evidence	Organization for Matter and Energy Flow in Organisms	Energy and Matter
	10	Develop a model to describe the movement of matter among plants, animals, decomposers, and the environment.	Developing and Using Models; Science Models, Laws, Mechanisms, and Theories Explain Natural Phenomena	Interdependent Relationships in Ecosystems; Cycles of Matter and Energy Transfer in Ecosystems	Systems and System Models
	11	Develop a model to describe the movement of matter among plants, animals, decomposers, and the environment.	Developing and Using Models; Science Models, Laws, Mechanisms, and Theories Explain Natural Phenomena	Interdependent Relationships in Ecosystems; Cycles of Matter and Energy Transfer in Ecosystems	Systems and System Models
	12	Develop a model to describe the movement of matter among plants, animals, decomposers, and the environment.	Developing and Using Models; Science Models, Laws, Mechanisms, and Theories Explain Natural Phenomena	Interdependent Relationships in Ecosystems; Cycles of Matter and Energy Transfer in Ecosystems	Systems and System Models
Physical	1	Develop a model to describe that matter is made of particles too small to be seen.	Developing and Using Models	Structure and Properties of Matter	Scale, Proportion, and Quantity
	2	Develop a model to describe that matter is made of particles too small to be seen.	Developing and Using Models	Structure and Properties of Matter	Scale, Proportion, and Quantity

Standards Correlations *(cont.)*

Unit	Week	Next Generation Science Standards			
		Performance Expectation	**Science and Engineering Practices**	**Disciplinary Core Ideas**	**Cross-Cutting Concepts**
Physical Science	3	Develop a model to describe that matter is made of particles too small to be seen.	Developing and Using Models	Structure and Properties of Matter	Scale, Proportion, and Quantity
	4	Measure and graph quantities to provide evidence that regardless of the type of change that occurs when heating, cooling, or mixing substances, the total weight of matter is conserved.	Using Mathematics and Computational Thinking	Structure and Properties of Matter Chemical Reactions	Scale, Proportion, and Quantity Scientific Knowledge Assumes an Order and Consistency in Natural Systems
	5	Measure and graph quantities to provide evidence that regardless of the type of change that occurs when heating, cooling, or mixing substances, the total weight of matter is conserved.	Using Mathematics and Computational Thinking	Structure and Properties of Matter Chemical Reactions	Scale, Proportion, and Quantity Scientific Knowledge Assumes an Order and Consistency in Natural Systems
	6	Make observations and measurements to identify materials based on their properties.	Planning and Carrying Out Investigations	Structure and Properties of Matter	Scale, Proportion, and Quantity
	7	Make observations and measurements to identify materials based on their properties.	Planning and Carrying Out Investigations	Structure and Properties of Matter	Scale, Proportion, and Quantity
	8	Conduct an investigation to determine whether the mixing of two or more substances results in new substances.	Planning and Carrying Out Investigations	Chemical Reactions	Cause and Effect
	9	Conduct an investigation to determine whether the mixing of two or more substances results in new substances.	Planning and Carrying Out Investigations	Chemical Reactions	Cause and Effect
	10	Use models to describe that energy in animals' food was once energy from the sun.	Developing and Using Models	Energy in Chemical Processes and Everyday Life Organization for Matter and Energy Flow in Organisms	Energy and Matter
	11	Use models to describe that energy in animals' food was once energy from the sun.	Developing and Using Models	Energy in Chemical Processes and Everyday Life Organization for Matter and Energy Flow in Organisms	Energy and Matter
	12	Support an argument that the gravitational force exerted by Earth on objects is directed down.	Engaging in Argument from Evidence	Types of Interactions	Cause and Effect
Earth and Space	1	Develop a model using an example to describe ways the geosphere, biosphere, hydrosphere, and/or atmosphere interact.	Developing and Using Models	Earth Materials and Systems	Systems and System Models
	2	Develop a model using an example to describe ways the geosphere, biosphere, hydrosphere, and/or atmosphere interact.	Developing and Using Models	Earth Materials and Systems	Systems and System Models

Standards Correlations *(cont.)*

Unit	Week	Performance Expectation	Science and Engineering Practices	Disciplinary Core Ideas	Cross-Cutting Concepts
		Next Generation Science Standards			
Earth and Space Science	3	Describe and graph the amounts and percentages of water and fresh water in various reservoirs to provide evidence about the distribution of water on Earth.	Using Mathematics and Computational Thinking	The Roles of Water in Earth's Surface	Scale, Proportion, and Quantity
	4	Describe and graph the amounts and percentages of water and fresh water in various reservoirs to provide evidence about the distribution of water on Earth.	Using Mathematics and Computational Thinking	The Roles of Water in Earth's Surface	Scale, Proportion, and Quantity
	5	Obtain and combine information about ways individual communities use science ideas to protect the Earth's resources and environment.	Obtaining, Evaluating, and Communicating Information	Human Impacts on Earth Systems	Systems and System Models Science Addresses Questions About the Natural and Material World
	6	Obtain and combine information about ways individual communities use science ideas to protect the Earth's resources and environment.	Obtaining, Evaluating, and Communicating Information	Human Impacts on Earth Systems	Systems and System Models Science Addresses Questions About the Natural and Material World
	7	Represent data in graphical displays to reveal patterns of daily changes in length and direction of shadows, day and night, and the seasonal appearance of some stars in the night sky.	Obtaining, Evaluating, and Communicating Information	Earth and the Solar System	Patterns
	8	Represent data in graphical displays to reveal patterns of daily changes in length and direction of shadows, day and night, and the seasonal appearance of some stars in the night sky.	Obtaining, Evaluating, and Communicating Information	Earth and the Solar System	Patterns
	9	Support an argument that differences in the apparent brightness of the sun compared to other stars is due to their relative distances from Earth.	Engaging in Argument from Evidence	The Universe and Its Stars	Scale, Proportion, and Quantity
	10	Represent data in graphical displays to reveal patterns of daily changes in length and direction of shadows, day and night, and the seasonal appearance of some stars in the night sky.	Analyzing and Interpreting Data	Earth and the Solar System	Patterns
	11	Represent data in graphical displays to reveal patterns of daily changes in length and direction of shadows, day and night, and the seasonal appearance of some stars in the night sky.	Analyzing and Interpreting Data	Earth and the Solar System	Patterns
	12	Represent data in graphical displays to reveal patterns of daily changes in length and direction of shadows, day and night, and the seasonal appearance of some stars in the night sky.	Analyzing and Interpreting Data	Earth and the Solar System	Patterns

Learning Content

Name: _____ **Date:** _____

Directions: Read the text, and answer the questions.

Life Cycles

Each plant and animal has a life cycle. A life cycle is the series of stages that all living things experience as they grow up and make new life. Life cycles are different. The differences depend on how long the plant or animal lives and the way they make new life. Life cycles are how life on Earth continues. When the last specimen of a plant or animal completes its life cycle without leaving offspring, we say that species is extinct.

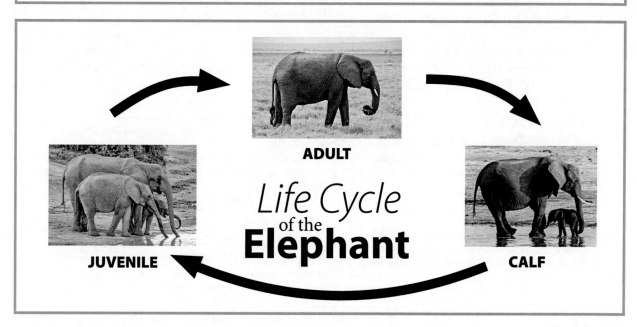

Life Cycle of the Elephant
ADULT
JUVENILE
CALF

1. What is the definition of a life cycle?

   a. the daily life of a plant or animal
   b. the stages all living things pass through
   c. something only animals experience
   d. the stages of the life of a plant

2. If there are no more specimens of a plant or animal left, we say the species is

   _____ .

   a. hibernating
   b. at the beginning of its life cycle
   c. extinct
   d. at the end of its life cycle

3. Why are the life cycles of plants and animals different?

   _____

   _____

Name: _____ **Date:** _____

Directions: Study the infographic, and answer the questions.

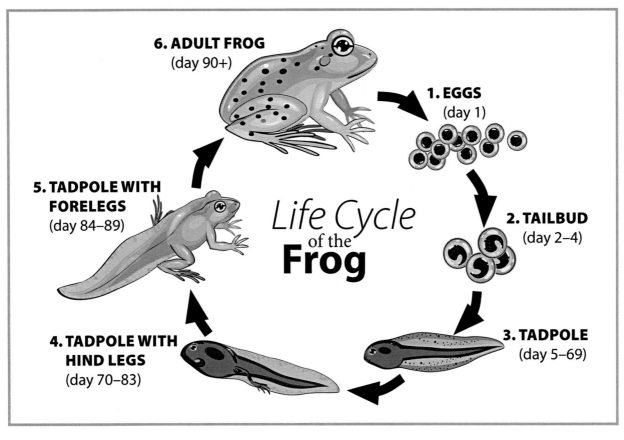

6. ADULT FROG
(day 90+)

1. EGGS
(day 1)

5. TADPOLE WITH FORELEGS
(day 84–89)

Life Cycle
of the
Frog

2. TAILBUD
(day 2–4)

4. TADPOLE WITH HIND LEGS
(day 70–83)

3. TADPOLE
(day 5–69)

1. How can you tell when a frog is an adult?

   a. It has a large tail.   **b.** It has a small tail.

   c. It has no tail.   **d.** It has legs.

2. How long does it take a frog to develop from an egg to an adult?

   a. about one week   **b.** about three weeks

   c. about three months   **d.** about a year

3. Describe the differences between stages 2 and 5 in frog's life cycle.

_____

_____

_____

_____

Developing Questions

Name: _____ **Date:** _____

Directions: Look at the illustration, and read the text. Then, answer the questions.

Martine is very interested in studying insects. She researches the life cycles of insects and discovers that they all go through the same stages. The stages are: egg, larva, pupa, and adult. These changes are called metamorphosis. The time these changes take varies for each type of insect.

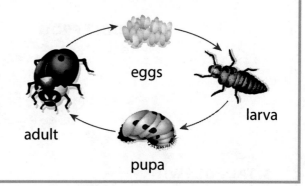

eggs

larva

adult

pupa

1. If Martine finds a butterfly cocoon in her back yard, what will she need to know if she wants to see the butterfly emerge?

   a. what the temperature was on the day the cocoon was formed

   b. how long it takes a butterfly to complete its metamorphosis

   c. what color the butterfly will be

   d. what food the butterfly will eat when it emerges

2. Martine finds some insect eggs on a leaf. If she comes back the next day and sees tiny bugs where the eggs were, what stage of the life cycle are the bugs most likely in?

   a. pupa

   b. adult

   c. larva

   d. molting

3. What is a question that Martine could ask to learn more about the process of metamorphosis?

   _____

   _____

4. Write about a time you saw a bug that was not fully grown.

   _____

   _____

Name: _____ **Date:** _____

Directions: Read the text, and answer the questions.

> Mammals grow inside their mothers during the first part of their life cycles. This is called pregnancy. Another name for this is the gestation period. Julian visits a farm and sees a pregnant cow and a pregnant pig. The farmer tells Julian that the gestation period for cows is 279 days, and the gestation period for pigs is 114 days.
>
>

Planning Solutions

1. Julian wants to see the baby cow once it is born. What important fact must he know?

   a. how long the cow has been pregnant

   b. what color the baby cow will be

   c. how long the gestation period is

   d. both a and c

2. The farmer tells Julian that the pig has been pregnant for 100 days. When should he come back to see the baby pigs?

   a. 3 months

   b. 2 months

   c. 1 week

   d. 2 weeks

3. What can Julian do to investigate which farm animals have the longest and shortest gestation periods?

   _____

   _____

   _____

Name: _____ Date: _____

Directions: Read the text, and complete the animal gestation graph.

Mammals grow inside their mothers during the first part of the life cycle. This is called pregnancy. Another name for this is the gestation period.

Communicating Results

Name of Animal	Gestation Period (days)
human	275
wolf	65
sheep	150
horse	336
elephant	624
giraffe	430

Animal Gestation Period

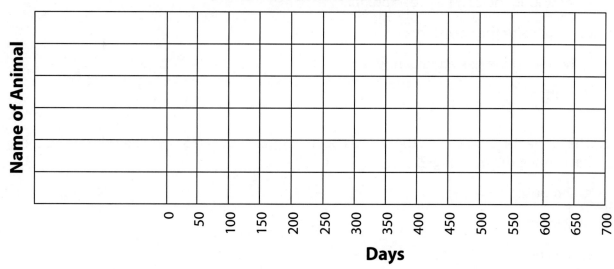

Days

1. Which animal has the shortest gestation? Which animal has the longest?

_____

_____

_____

Name: _____ Date: _____

Directions: Read the text, and answer the questions.

The Life Cycle of Humans

All humans go through a life cycle. You began growing inside your mother. After about nine months, you were born as a baby. You will go through many stages of life. You have already gone through the infancy/toddler stage. Now you are in childhood. Next comes adolescence, young adulthood, middle adulthood, and late adulthood. Your body changes in each stage. You have already gone through many changes. You have many more exciting changes ahead of you.

1. How many life cycle stages do humans go through?

   a. 3   b. 5

   c. 6   d. 7

2. Each stage of the human life cycle _____ .

   a. lasts the same length of time   b. is very similar to the one before

   c. is marked by many changes   d. is different for each person

3. Which two stages do you think are the most different from each other, and why?

   _____

   _____

Name: _____ **Date:** _____

Directions: Read the text, and study the infographic. Answer the questions.

A human goes through more changes in the first year of life than at any other time. The illustrations show a major milestone for each month of the first year of life.

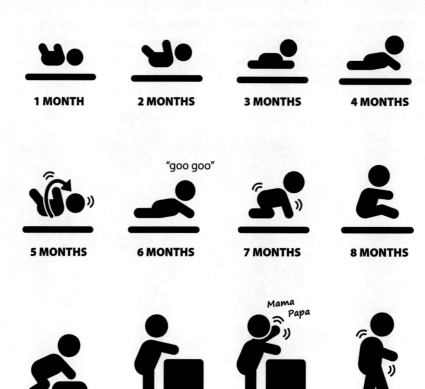

1 MONTH   2 MONTHS   3 MONTHS   4 MONTHS

"goo goo"

5 MONTHS   6 MONTHS   7 MONTHS   8 MONTHS

Mama Papa

9 MONTHS   10 MONTHS   11 MONTHS   12 MONTHS

1. Most babies first roll over at _____ .

   a. birth   **b.** 2 months

   c. 3 months   **d.** 5 months

2. What can most babies do at 12 months that they couldn't do at 11 months?

   a. talk   **b.** stand up

   c. walk   **d.** crawl

3. What do you think is the hardest skill for a baby to learn?

_____

_____

Name: _____ **Date:** _____

Directions: Read the text. Answer the questions.

> The human life cycle stages are based on changes you can observe. The changes occur in both the body and the mind. Everyone goes through the same stages in the same order. The stages roughly correspond to a person's age, but they are not precise. Some people go through certain stages a little bit faster or slower than other people.
>
> • Infancy and toddlerhood: birth until about age 4
> • Childhood: about ages 4 to 12
> • Adolescence: about ages 12 to 22
> • Young adult: about ages 22 to 40
> • Middle adulthood: about ages 40 to 55
> • Later adulthood: about ages 55 on

Developing Questions

1. Juan is 12½ years old. How can you tell if he is still in childhood or if he is entering adolescence?

   a. by how much he weighs   **b.** by his grade in school

   c. by his birthday   **d.** by physical changes

2. If a person lives to be 75 years old, which three life stages make up the majority of that person's life?

   a. infancy/toddlerhood, childhood, adolescence
   b. young adulthood, middle adulthood, later adulthood

   c. childhood, adolescence, young adulthood
   d. adolescence, young adulthood, middle adulthood

3. What is a question you have about life cycle stages?

   _____

   _____

   _____

Planning Solutions

Name: _____ **Date:** _____

Directions: Read the text and then answer the questions.

Alexis is ten years old and has a five-year-old brother. You tell her that both she and her brother are in the same life cycle stage: childhood. She doesn't feel like she is in the same stage as her brother. She says she knows a lot more than her brother. She argues that she is much taller than her brother. She also says she is older than her brother.

1. Which mistake does Alexis make when she thinks about her life cycle stage?

   a. She thinks that age is the good way to tell a life cycle stage.

   b. She thinks that height is a good way to tell a life cycle stage.

   c. She thinks that knowledge is a good way to tell a life cycle stage.

   d. all of the above

2. How could you explain to Alexis that she really still is in childhood?

   a. You could say that she hasn't passed the test to enter adolescence yet.

   b. You could say that there are many differences in the same stages.

   c. You could say that childhood lasts until adults say you've grown up.

   d. You could say that she has to be exactly 12 years old before she can be in a different life cycle.

3. What could Alexis do to understand more about the childhood stage?

   _____

   _____

   _____

   _____

51411—180 Days of Science

Name: _____ **Date:** _____

Directions: This chart is for members of your family. Fill out as much of it as you can by writing names of your family members on the lines. Label the different stages of the life cycle.

Grandpa	Grandma		Grandpa	Grandma
_____	_____		_____	_____

	Dad		Mom	
	_____		_____	

Child	Child	Child	Child
_____	_____	_____	_____

1. Which members of your family are in the same stages of the life cycle?

_____

_____

_____

2. Write something you'd like to share about your family tree.

_____

_____

Communicating Results

Name: _____ **Date:** _____

Directions: Read the text, and answer the questions.

The Life Cycle of Reptiles

Snakes and lizards are reptiles. Alligators and turtles are reptiles, too. All reptiles go through similar stages in their life cycles. The stages are egg, hatchling, juvenile, and adult. Many hatchlings and juveniles look just like tiny adults. However, they are much, much smaller!

Mothers usually bury their eggs in loose soil or sand. The number of eggs varies greatly by species. Some reptiles lay only one or two eggs, while others lay 100 or more. They typically do not stay with their young. When they hatch, the animals are on their own.

1. Which one of the following is **not** a reptile?

   a. snake

   b. frog

   c. lizard

   d. turtle

2. All reptiles _____ .

   a. live in water

   b. have many teeth

   c. have hair

   d. have a hatchling stage

3. What are some ways a reptile's life cycle is different from your life cycle?

   _____

   _____

   _____

51411—180 Days of Science

Name: _____ Date: _____

Directions: Study the infographic, and answer the questions.

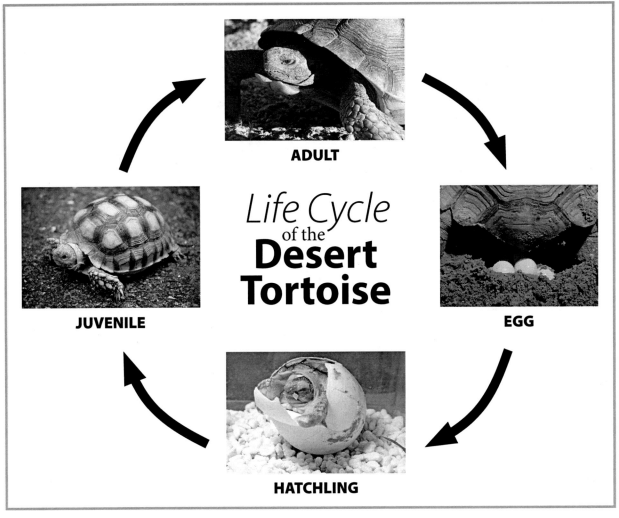

1. The desert tortoise looks the most different from an adult in its _____ stage.

   a. egg

   b. hatchling

   c. juvenile

   d. crawling

2. How can you tell the difference between a juvenile tortoise and an adult?

   a. their size

   b. their voice

   c. their feet

   d. their eyes

3. In which stage would the tortoise make a nest for eggs? How do you know?

   _____

   _____

Name: _____ **Date:** _____

Directions: Read the text, and answer the questions.

A sea turtle comes out of the ocean and digs in the sand to create a nest. She then goes back into the ocean and swims out to sea. About four months later, small turtles start coming out of the sand and immediately head toward the ocean.

1. What was the sea turtle doing when she dug in the sand?

   a. making a bed

   b. looking for food

   c. building a nest

   d. drying off from the water

2. When the turtles start coming out of the sand, in which stage of the life cycle are they?

   a. egg

   b. hatchling

   c. adult

   d. toddler

3. Write something you'd like to ask about the small turtles that come out of the sand.

   _____

   _____

   _____

4. What do you think happens when the small turtles go back to the ocean?

   _____

   _____

   _____

Developing Questions

Planning Solutions

Name: _____ **Date:** _____

Directions: Read the text, and answer the questions.

Some reptiles make interesting pets. Jose has a pet bearded dragon. It is 45 centimeters long. Adult bearded dragons range in size from 30 to 60 centimeters. Like other reptiles, they grow bigger as they get older, but they also get bigger depending on how much food they eat. In addition, the bigger the cage they live in, the bigger they can grow. They can grow up to 60 centimeters (24 inches).

1. Jose's friend has a dragon that is 20 cm long. Is it a juvenile or an adult?

   a. Adult, because it is done growing.

   b. Juvenile, because adults are 20–60 cm.

   c. Adult, because it is still growing.

   d. Juvenile, because adults are 30–60 cm.

2. What does Jose need to do to make sure his dragon grows as big as possible?

   a. Wait for it to get older.

   b. Make sure it has lots of food.

   c. Put it in a big tank.

   d. all of the above

3. What can Jose do to find out if his dragon is finished growing?

   _____

   _____

   _____

4. What are some other reptiles you could keep as pets?

   _____

   _____

Name: _____   Date: _____

Directions: Study the chart. Complete the graph to show the average lifespans of different reptiles.

Name of Animal	Length of Life
alligator	35 years
desert tortoise	80 years
corn snake	7 years
python	15 years
gecko	20 years
chameleon	3 years
turtle	50 years

Average Lifespans of Reptiles

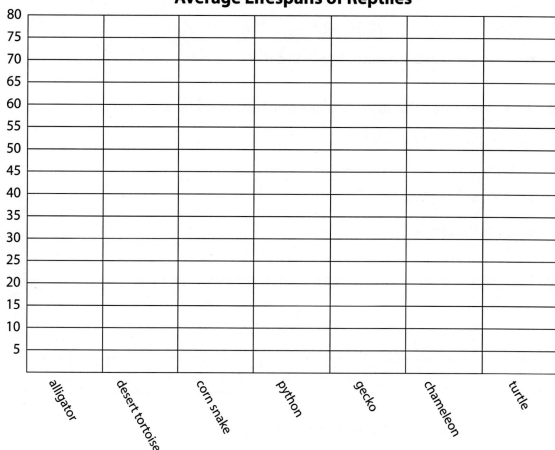

Name: _____ Date: _____

Directions: Read the text, and answer the questions.

Vertebrates and Invertebrates

Many animals have backbones. These animals are called vertebrates. Dogs, cats, birds, fish, and humans are all examples of vertebrates. Vertebrates have skeletons made of bone or cartilage. They live in all habitats on Earth. Those that live on land are called terrestrial animals. Those that live in the water are called aquatic animals.

Animals without backbones are called invertebrates. They often have shells or hard outer coverings that help protect them. These coverings are called exoskeletons. They are hard but have joints that allow the animal to move. Spiders, bugs, and worms are invertebrates you might see outside.

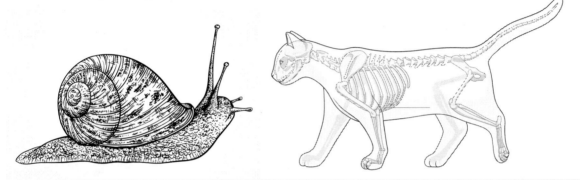

1. What do vertebrates have that invertebrates don't have?

   a. legs

   b. wings

   c. backbone

   d. tail

2. Vertebrates _____ .

   a. live only on land

   b. live only in the water

   c. live on land and in the water

   d. live in all habitats

3. What are some common types of vertebrates?

   _____

   _____

Analyzing Data

Name: _____ **Date:** _____

Directions: Read the text. Then, study the diagram, and answer the questions.

Both vertebrates and invertebrates live in many different places. Vertebrates have backbones, and invertebrates usually have hard outer coverings. Some animals live primarily on land, and some animals live primarily in the water. There are also animals who live both in water and on land.

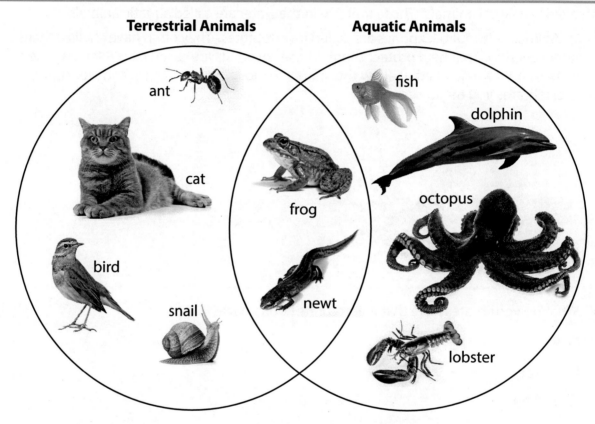

Terrestrial Animals   **Aquatic Animals**

ant

fish

dolphin

cat

frog

octopus

bird

snail

newt

lobster

1. Which of the terrestrial animals in the diagram are invertebrates?

   a. birds and cats

   b. snails and birds

   c. ants and cats

   d. snails and ants

2. What do frogs and fish have in common?

   a. They spend time in the water.

   b. They have fur.

   c. They spend time on land.

   d. They are have legs.

3. What is one major difference between frogs and cats?

   _____

   _____

51411—180 Days of Science

Name: _____ **Date:** _____

Directions: Read the text, and answer the questions.

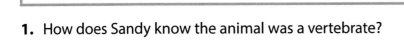

Sandy is a paleontologist. Paleontologists are scientists who study fossils. Fossils are the remains of ancient animals. They are sometimes found at dig sites. Fossils can help us understand many things about ancient animals. Sandy uncovers a new fossil while working at a dig site. She finds part of a leg, a backbone, a piece of skull, and a tooth.

Developing Questions

1. How does Sandy know the animal was a vertebrate?

   a. All ancient creatures were vertebrates.

   b. Invertebrates never have legs.

   c. She found a backbone.

   d. She can tell from the area where she dug up the bones.

2. How does the piece of skull help prove that the animal was a vertebrate?

   a. because the skull is part of a skeleton

   b. because the skull is made of bone

   c. It doesn't help prove it.

   d. both a and b

3. Since Sandy can tell that the fossil is from a vertebrate, what is a question she might ask about the fossil to learn more about it?

   _____

   _____

   _____

   _____

Planning Solutions

Name: _____ **Date:** _____

Directions: Read the text, and answer the questions.

Lobsters, grasshoppers, and crabs all have exoskeletons. This means their hard, outer coverings protect their soft tissues on the inside.

Ana wants to make a model of a lobster for the science fair.

1. What characteristics of an exoskeleton should Ana's model demonstrate?

    a. It is hard but does not bend.

    b. It is soft and bends at joints.

    c. It is hard and bends at joints.

    d. It is soft and does not bend.

2. Which material would be best for Ana to use in her model exoskeleton?

    a. pipe cleaners bundled together

    b. shoe boxes linked together with stuffing inside

    c. a cardboard box with stuffing glued to the outside

    d. sticks bundled together

3. Ana decides to build a model of a vertebrate instead. How would she need to change her model?

    _____

    _____

    _____

    _____

Name: _____ **Date:** _____

Directions: Label each animal with "vertebrate" or "invertebrate" and "terrestrial" or "aquatic."

lion

snake

shark

jellyfish

lizard

bee

tick

tuna

clam

pigeon

ladybug

octopus

Communicating Results

ABC

Name: _____ Date: _____

Directions: Read the text, and answer the questions.

Human Traits

Everyone is unique. The things that make us unique are called traits. Traits are characteristics. We may share traits with other people, but we all have a unique combination. Some traits are inherited, or passed from parent to child. Eye color, hair color, and even the ability to roll your tongue are all inherited.

We acquire some characteristics through learning or the effects of the environment. This could be your ability to ride a bike or play an instrument. You are not born with these things like you are with inherited traits.

 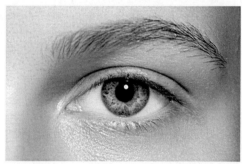

1. Which is an example of an inherited trait?

   a. ability to ride a bike
   b. ability to play an instrument
   c. manners
   d. eye color

2. Where do inherited traits come from?

   a. parents
   b. children
   c. pets
   d. the environment

3. How can you acquire a new characteristic?

   a. learn a new skill
   b. be born with blue eyes
   c. eat a new food
   d. be born with dark skin

4. Is it possible for you to have the exact same traits as one of your parents? Why or why not?

   _____

   _____

   _____

Name: _____ **Date:** _____

Directions: Read the text, and study the chart. Then, answer the questions.

If you inherit a trait, it was passed down to you from your parents. You can pass down an inherited trait to your children. Acquired traits are not passed down genetically. The only way you can acquire them is through learning or the effects of the environment.

Analyzing Data

Trait	Inherited or Acquired
eye color	inherited
calluses on fingers	acquired
large muscles from exercise	acquired
hair color	inherited
ability to ride a bike	acquired
dimples	inherited

1. Which is an acquired trait?

  a. dimples

  b. hair color

  c. ability to ride a bike

  d. eye color

2. Which is an inherited trait

  a. dimples

  b. large muscles from exercise

  c. ability to ride a bike

  d. calluses on fingers

3. If you break your leg, would that be passed down to your children?

  a. Yes, it would be passed down genetically.

  b. Yes, the child would learn this characteristic.

  c. No, acquired traits are not passed down genetically.

  d. No, both parents would have to break their legs for it to pass down.

Developing Questions

Name: _____ **Date:** _____

Directions: Read the text, and answer the questions.

Almost no one can tell Stacey and her identical twin sister, Jen, apart. Their likeness is uncanny. They both have curly hair, brown eyes, and fair skin. There is one way people can tell them apart, though. Stacey knows how to play the flute, and Jen knows how to play the trumpet, but neither knows how to play the other instrument.

1. Why do identical twins look alike?

    a. They inherited all the same traits.

    b. They inherited different traits.

    c. They inherited some of the same traits.

    d. They have the same haircut.

2. How could you tell Stacey and Jen apart?

    a. Ask them to stand side by side.

    b. Ask to hear their voices.

    c. Check to see who's taller.

    d. Ask them to play the flute.

3. What could you ask about identical twins and other sibings?

    _____

    _____

    _____

4. Do you think it would be hard to tell identical twins apart? Why or why not?

    _____

    _____

Name: _____ Date: _____

Directions: Read the text. Answer the questions.

Stacey's eyes are brown, and so are her identical twin sister's. Their mother's eyes are brown, too, but their father's eyes are blue. The whole family has curly hair. Stacey wants to know how she can have different colored eyes from her father.

1. Who did Stacey inherit her brown eyes from?

   a. mother

   b. father

   c. sister

   d. brother

2. Who did Stacey inherit her curly hair from?

   a. parents

   b. sister

   c. brother

   d. no one

3. How can Stacey find out where her dad got his blue eyes?

   _____

   _____

   _____

4. Do you look like anyone else in your family? If so, how?

   _____

   _____

Planning Solutions

Communicating Results

Name: _____ Date: _____

Directions: Study the picture, and label the traits as "inherited" or "acquired." Then, answer the questions.

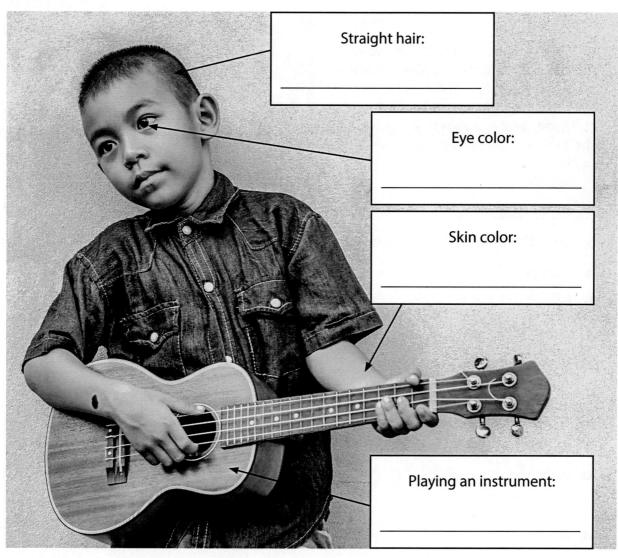

Straight hair:

_____

Eye color:

_____

Skin color:

_____

Playing an instrument:

_____

1. What are some acquired traits you have?

_____

_____

_____

2. What are some inherited traits you have?

_____

_____

Name: _____ **Date:** _____

Learning Content

Directions: Read the text, and answer the questions.

Animal Behavior

Heredity is when a trait is passed down from parents to children. In animals, instincts are the result of heredity. An instinct is something that an animal is born knowing how to do. Instincts help animals survive in their environments. Many birds migrate south is because of instinct.

Other behaviors are learned. Animals usually learn behaviors from their parents. They can learn behaviors from people, too. Dolphins are born knowing how to swim, but they can learn to do tricks. A dog is born knowing how to chase things, but a dog playing fetch is a learned behavior.

1. Which is an example of an instinct?

   a. a dog playing fetch

   b. birds migrating

   c. dolphins doing tricks

   d. horses racing on a track

2. Which is an example of a learned behavior?

   a. a parrot saying, "Hello"

   b. a fish swimming

   c. birds migrating

   d. a bee building a hive

3. Why are instincts important to animals?

   _____

   _____

   _____

   _____

Analyzing Data

Name: _____ **Date:** _____

Directions: Read the text, and study the chart. Then, answer the questions.

> While animals have many instinctual behaviors, they are also able to learn how to do things. If you have a pet, you may have trained it to do certain things. These are learned behaviors.

Behavior	Instinct or Learned
playing fetch	learned
building a nest	instinct
spinning a web	instinct
saying human words	learned
doing tricks	learned
sucking water into trunk	instinct

1. Which animal behavior is learned?

   a. building a nest

   b. sucking water into a trunk

   c. spinning a web

   d. saying human words

2. Which animal behavior is an instinct?

   a. spinning a web

   b. playing fetch

   c. saying human words

   d. doing tricks

Name: _____ **Date:** _____

Directions: Read the text, and answer the questions.

Aiden sees a bird in the tree outside his bedroom window. It flies away and brings back some twigs. After arranging them on a branch, it flies away and brings back more twigs. The bird repeats this process over time until it has instinctually built a nest for its new home.

1. How does the bird know how to build a nest?

    a. learning

    b. instinct

    c. guessing

    d. luck

2. What would happen if the nest was destroyed?

    a. The bird would build a new nest in the tree.

    b. The bird would decide to live without a nest.

    c. The bird would make a nest in the grass.

    d. The bird would make a nest underground.

3. What could Aiden ask about the bird's behavior?

_____

_____

_____

4. Write about a time you have seen an animal doing something because of instinct.

_____

_____

Planning Solutions

Name: _____ **Date:** _____

Directions: Read the text, and answer the questions.

Olivia has a new puppy named Sparky. She likes to throw a ball to Sparky, but he just runs away with it. The next time she throws it, she holds out a treat so that he will bring it back. She does this several times until Sparky learns to always bring back the ball. Eventually, he brings it back on his own, even when she doesn't have any treats.

1. How did Sparky know how to play fetch?

   a. It was instinct.

   b. He learned from Olivia.

   c. He learned from his dad.

   d. His learned from his mom.

2. Why did Sparky bring the ball back at first?

   a. He got a treat.

   b. Olivia asked him nicely.

   c. He knew they were playing fetch.

   d. He wanted to.

3. How might Olivia teach Sparky to sit?

   _____

   _____

   _____

4. What else could Olivia teach Sparky?

   _____

   _____

Name: _____ **Date:** _____

Directions: List learned behaviors and instincts for cat and dogs. Then, answer the questions.

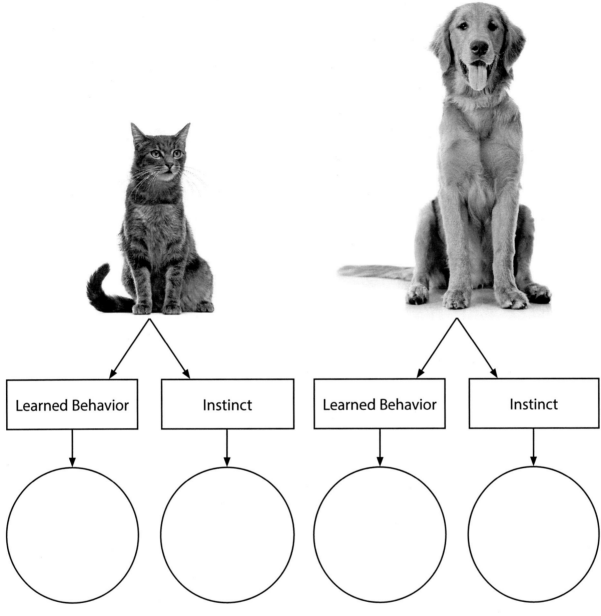

| Learned Behavior | Instinct | Learned Behavior | Instinct |

1. Have you ever taught an animal something? If so, what?

_____

_____

2. List a learned behavior and an instinct for another animal, such as a parakeet.

_____

_____

Communicating Results

Learning Content

Name: _____   Date: _____

Directions: Read the text, and answer the questions.

Food Chains

Plants, animals, and humans are all part of ecosystems. Ecosystems are living things and their environments. Living things in an ecosystem depend on each other to meet their needs. Every ecosystem has one or more food chains. A food chain is the order in which each living thing gets food. It shows how energy is passed from creature to creature.

Food chains begin with plants, which make their own food. Plants are eaten by animals, and then those animals are eaten by other animals. One example of a food chain would be clover, a rabbit, a fox, and a worm. The rabbit would eat the clover, and then the fox would eat the rabbit. When the fox dies, the worm would help the fox's body decompose. This puts nutrients in the soil, which helps more clovers grow.

1. What is an ecosystem?

   a. a food chain

   b. living things and their environment

   c. a group of plants

   d. a group of animals

2. What is a food chain?

   a. a community of living things

   b. a bird catching a fish

   c. the order in which living things get food and pass energy

   d. how humans, plants, and animals interact

3. How does a worm function in a food chain?

   a. It eats living plants and animals.

   b. It decomposes dead plants and animals.

   c. It makes its own food.

   d. It is not part of a food chain.

4. What is an example of a food chain?

   _____

   _____

Name: _____ Date: _____

Directions: Read the text, and study the food chain. Answer the questions.

> Food chains start with producers. A producer is an organism that produces its own food, like a plant. Next are primary consumers, which eat the producers. Secondary consumers eat the primary consumers. Finally, there are decomposers. They eat decaying matter and release nutrients back into the soil or ocean.

Analyzing Data

Food Chain

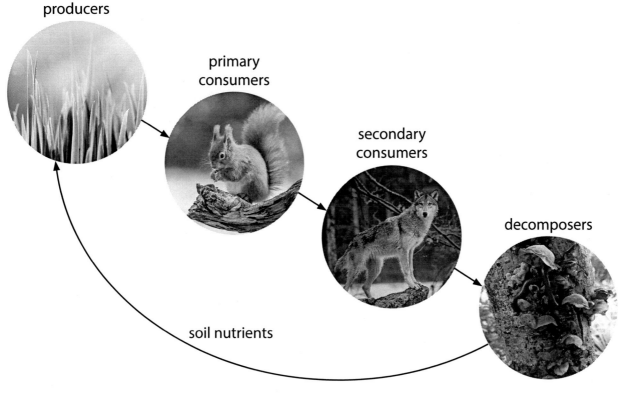

producers

primary consumers

secondary consumers

decomposers

soil nutrients

1. Where in the food chain are plants?

   a. first   **b.** second

   c. third   **d.** fourth

2. What are the animals that eat the plants called?

   a. decomposers   **b.** producers

   c. primary consumers   **d.** secondary consumers

3. What are the animals that eat the primary consumers called?

   a. secondary consumers   **b.** producers

   c. decomposers   **d.** primary consumers

Developing Questions

Name: _____ **Date:** _____

Directions: Read the text, and study the food chain. Then, answer the questions.

There are many plants around a pond. The plants are producers, and they all make their own food using air, water, nutrients from the soil, and energy from sunlight. Grasshoppers are consumers, and they eat the plants to get energy. Frogs eat the grasshoppers, and snakes eat the frogs. Energy starts with the plants and flows through the food chain.

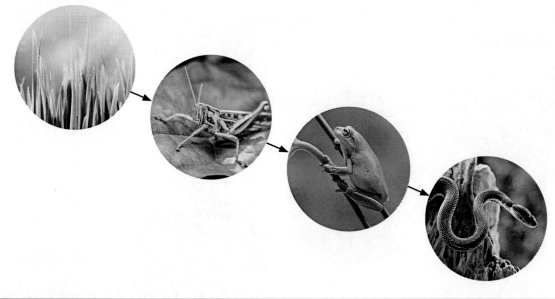

1. Which way is the energy flowing?

   a. from the grass to the grasshopper

   b. from the frog to the grasshopper

   c. from the snake to the grass

   d. from the grasshopper to the grass

2. Can plants get energy from grasshoppers?

   a. Yes, they can eat them.

   b. Yes, they can absorb it.

   c. No, they make their own food.

   d. No, plants don't need energy.

3. What is a question you can ask about this food chain?

   _____

   _____

   _____

   _____

Name: _____ **Date:** _____

Directions: Read the text, and answer the questions.

Every living thing needs food. Food may be used for many things, including growing, healing staying warm, or moving. A food chain is the order in which each living thing gets food and how energy is passed from creature to creature. A food web is a system of food chains that interact with each other. Food webs exist because most organisms consume more than one type of plant or animal.

Food Web

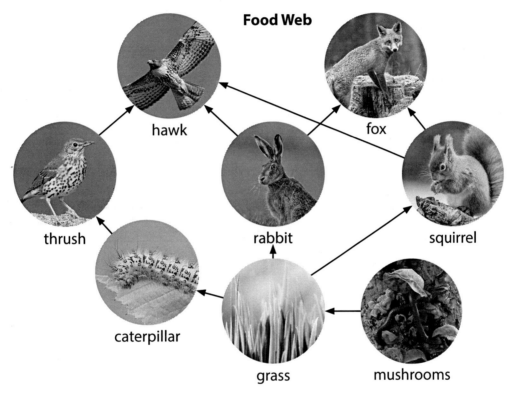

1. Which animals are primary consumers?

   a. fox and thrush

   b. hawk and fox

   c. caterpillar and squirrel

   d. mushrooms and thrush

2. Which animals eat the squirrel?

   a. fox and hawk

   b. caterpillar and hawk

   c. hawk and rabbit

   d. fox and caterpillar

3. How can you explore food webs in a park or your backyard?

   _____

   _____

Planning Solutions

Communicating Results

Name: _____ Date: _____

Directions: Complete the chart with the correct stages of the food chain from the word bank. Then, answer the questions.

| decomposer | primary consumer | producer | secondary consumer |

Food Chain

clover
_____

↓

rabbit
_____

↓

fox
_____

↓

earthworm
_____

1. Where do you think you fit into the food chain? Why?

_____

_____

_____

2. Which stage of the food chain is important for recycling decaying plants and animals?

_____

Name: _____ **Date:** _____

Directions: Read the text, and answer the questions.

Food Chains in the Jungle

Jungles are teeming with life. There are many plants, insects, birds, frogs, snakes, lizards, and larger animals that call the jungle home. There are so many living things in a jungle that there are many food chains. A food chain is the order in which each living thing gets food and how energy is passed from creature to creature. Since most living things eat more than one type of plant or animal, the different food chains interact and form food webs.

An example of a jungle food chain is a banana tree, a monkey, and a jaguar. The monkey eats bananas, and the jaguar eats the monkey. In reality, this food chain is part of a more complex food web in which the monkey and the jaguar both eat other things as well.

Learning Content

1. What is passed between creatures in a food chain?

   a. sunlight
   b. energy
   c. water
   d. behaviors

2. Which organism could be added to the food chain described to create a food web?

   a. seals to eat the bananas
   b. pythons for the frog to eat
   c. fish for the jaguar to eat
   d. fish to eat the jaguar

3. You would not find _____ in a jungle food chain.

   a. jellyfish
   b. frogs
   c. monkeys
   d. plants

Analyzing Data

Name: _____ Date: _____

Directions: Read the text, and study the chart. Then, answer the questions.

> The energy source for all ecosystems is the sun. Energy moves through a food chain as one animal eats another animal or plant. It starts with producers.

	Organism Example	Food Source
Producer	banana tree	produce their own from air, water, and sunlight
Primary Consumer	monkey	plants
Secondary Consumer	jaguar	animals that eat plants
Decomposer	mushroom	decaying plants and animals

1. Where does the food chain start?

   a. decomposers
   b. primary consumers
   c. secondary consumers
   d. producers

2. Which organism in the chart eats the monkey?

   a. banana tree
   b. jaguar
   c. mushroom
   d. sun

3. Which organism breaks down dead plants and animals?

   a. mushroom
   b. plants
   c. monkey
   d. jaguar

Name: _____ **Date:** _____

Directions: Read the text, and look at the food web. Then, answer the questions.

> In a food web, different food chains interact with each other. In the jungle, different predators are competing for the same food sources. The jaguar and python compete for some of the same food.

Food Web

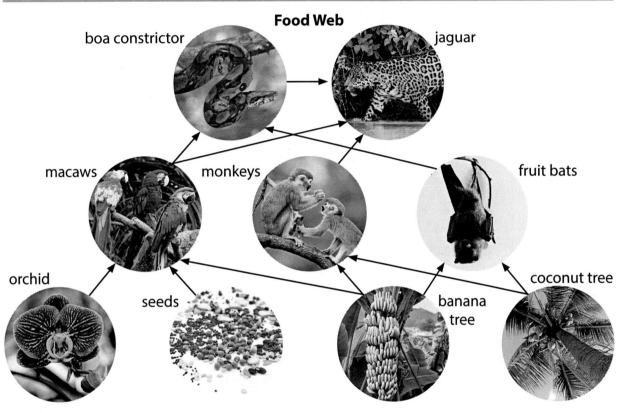

boa constrictor
jaguar
macaws
monkeys
fruit bats
orchid
seeds
banana tree
coconut tree

1. Where does energy from the banana tree flow next?

   a. to the jaguar, boa constrictor, and orchid

   b. to coconut trees, orchids, and macaws

   c. to macaws, monkeys, and fruit bats

   d. to seeds, monkeys, and fruit bats

2. Does the jaguar get energy straight from seeds?

   a. Yes, they eat seeds all the time.

   b. No, there are no seeds in their food chain.

   c. Yes, they eat seeds if they can't find monkeys.

   d. No, they eat animals that eat seeds.

3. What is a question you can ask about the food web?

   _____

Planning Solutions

Name: _____ **Date:** _____

Directions: Read the text, and answer the questions.

The jaguar and the boa constrictor compete for some of the same food sources. The jaguar doesn't usually have to worry about other animals eating it. It is at the top of the food chain. The boa constrictor does have to worry about a few other animals trying to eat it.

1. Which animal is at the top of its food chain?

   a. jaguar

   c. both

   b. boa constrictor

   d. neither

2. What does it mean to be at the top of the food chain?

   a. other animals don't try to eat it

   c. some other animals try to eat it

   b. all other animals try to eat it

   d. it competes for food

3. How can you find out if an animal is at the top of the food chain?

   _____

   _____

4. Do you think humans are at the top of their food chain? Why or why not?

   _____

   _____

Name: _____ **Date:** _____

Directions: Draw an organism in each box to create a simple food chain.

Food Chain

Producer

↓

Primary Consumer

↓

Secondary Consumer

↓

Decomposer

Communicating Results

ABC

Learning Content

Name: _____ Date: _____

Directions: Read the text, and answer the questions.

Plant Needs

Plants are unique because, unlike other organisms, they make their own food. In every food chain, they are called producers. Plants use water that they absorb from soil, carbon dioxide from air, and energy from the sun to make their food. This process is called photosynthesis.

Just like animals, plants need energy to grow. If plants do not have all the things they need, they cannot make their own food. Then, they cannot grow because they get energy to grow from the food they make. Because of plants, energy from the sun can be used by all animals on Earth. Excess energy is stored in different parts of the plant. The energy is stored as glucose, which is a type of sugar.

1. How do plants get food?

   a. They make it from water, air, and sun.

   b. They make it from water, sun, and animals.

   c. They don't need food.

   d. They make it from animals, sun, and rocks.

2. Where do plants get the energy they need to grow?

   a. bugs

   b. the food they make

   c. soil

   d. water

3. What do plants do with excess energy?

   a. digest it

   b. remove it

   c. share it

   d. store it

Name: _____ **Date:** _____

Directions: Plants A, B, and C are the same type of plant. Study the chart, and answer the questions.

Analyzing Data

	Plant A	Plant B	Plant C
Water given per week	2 cups	2 cups	1 cup
Sunlight	full sun	partial sun	full sun
Growth in two weeks	3 inches	2 inches	1 inch

1. What is affecting the growth of the plants?

    a. water

    b. air

    c. sunlight

    d. water and sunlight

2. What is the best combination of water and sunlight for this type of plant?

    a. two cups of water and full sun

    b. two cups of water and partial sun

    c. one cup of water and full sun

    d. one cup of water and partial sun

3. Since plant A grew the most, it made the most _____.

    a. food

    b. water

    c. air

    d. sun

Developing Questions

Name: _____ **Date:** _____

Directions: Read the text, and look at the pictures. Then, answer the questions.

Jamal is conducting an experiment to see how air affects plant growth. He has two plants. They each sit in a sunny area, and they each get water every two days. He covers one plant with a clear plastic bag, so it does not get any air.

Plant A

Plant B

1. Will both plants get what they need to make food?

   a. Yes, plants don't need air.

   b. No, plants need air.

   c. Yes, air can go through the plastic.

   d. No, the plastic keeps too much air in.

2. What could happen to Plant B if it doesn't get air for long enough?

   a. It will die.

   b. It will grow.

   c. It will make its own air.

   d. It will remove the bag.

3. What is a question Jamal can ask about how air will affect the plants?

   _____

   _____

   _____

Name: _____ Date: _____

Directions: Read the text, and answer the questions.

Jamal is experimenting with the way air affects plants. His hypothesis is that plants cannot live without air. He has two plants, both of which are in a sunny area and get water every two days. One plant is covered in a clear plastic bag. Eventually, the covered plant begins to wilt and turn brown.

Plant A   **Plant B**

1. Was Jamal's hypothesis correct?

   a. Yes, the covered plant is dying.

   b. No, it is normal for a healthy plant to turn brown.

   c. Yes, the covered plant is thriving.

   d. No, it is both plants look the same.

2. Why do the plants need air?

   a. to make food

   b. to breathe

   c. to stay cool

   d. to make wind

3. How could Jamal test the effects of water on plants?

_____

_____

Name: _____ **Date:** _____

Directions: Plants need air, water, and sunlight to make food. Add to the picture to show the things that the plant needs to make food. Label the things you draw.

Name: _____ Date: _____

Directions: Read the text, and answer the questions.

The Role of Decomposers

All living things need energy to live. Just like plants and animals, decomposers are living things that need energy, too. Decomposers are part of every food chain. They break down waste and plants and animals that have died. Then they put nutrients back into the soil or ocean. Plants use these nutrients, and they go back into the food chain. Mushrooms, worms, mold, and bacteria are all types of decomposers. Many living things would not exist without decomposers.

 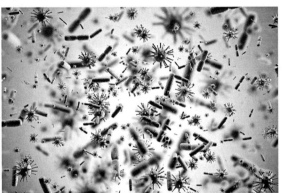

1. What breaks down dead plants and animals?

   a. soil

   b. oceans

   c. decomposers

   d. food chains

2. What are decomposers part of?

   a. food chains

   b. plants

   c. animals

   d. nutrients

3. Which organism is not a decomposer?

   a. mushroom

   b. worm

   c. bacteria

   d. hawk

4. What are some decomposers that you have seen outside?

   _____

   _____

Name: _____ Date: _____

Directions: Read the text, and study the chart. Then, answer the questions.

Simple Food Chain

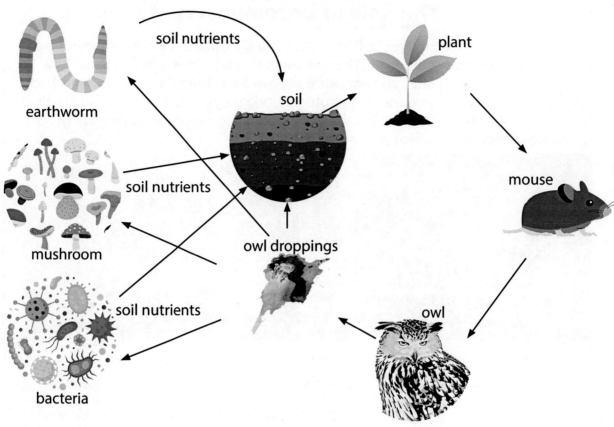

1. What are the decomposers breaking down?

    a. owl droppings   **b.** soil

    c. plant   **d.** owl

2. When the decomposers are done, where do the nutrients go next?

    a. into the plant   **b.** into the owl

    c. into the soil   **d.** into the mouse

3. What uses the nutrients that the decomposers put back into the food chain?

    a. mouse   **b.** plant

    c. owl   **d.** mushroom

Name: _____ **Date:** _____

Directions: Read the text, and answer the questions.

Mushrooms grow on a decaying tree stump. Nearby, worms are in the soil among dead tree leaves. After time, the tree stump is smaller, and the leaves are gone. New plants are growing nearby.

Developing Questions

1. Why did the tree stump get smaller?

    a. Water washed it away after time.

    b. It disintegrated because of wind.

    c. The mushrooms decomposed it.

    d. A bear gnawed it into a stump.

2. What is helping the new plants grow?

    a. Decomposers put nutrients back in the soil.

    b. Worms give the plants water.

    c. Mushrooms give the plants food.

    d. There is no way to tell.

3. What is a question you have about the decomposers you see outside?

_____

_____

_____

_____

Planning Solutions

Name: _____ **Date:** _____

Directions: Read the text, and answer the questions.

Dylan's mom has a compost pile in the backyard. Compost starts with organic matter, like scraps of fruit and vegetables. It decomposes and is recycled as fertilizer. The process requires some soil, water, and air. Bacteria from the soil, worms, and other organisms eat the organic matter. This breaks it down and raises the temperature of the compost pile. Then it turns it into fertilizer.

Dylan helps her mother add food scraps to the compost pile, mix it up, and water it. She often sees worms and bugs in the compost.

1. How do the fruit and vegetable scraps turn into fertilizer?

   a. Decomposers eat them.

   b. They are sent to a factory.

   c. They are put next to plants.

   d. They grow into new plants.

2. What are the worms doing in the compost?

   a. Lowering the temperature of the soil.

   b. Decomposing the organic matter.

   c. Adding water to the pile of scraps.

   d. Building nests to reproduce.

3. How could Dylan test to see what the worms do to the vegetable scraps?

   _____

   _____

   _____

   _____

51411—180 Days of Science   © *Shell Education*

Name: _____ **Date:** _____

Directions: Draw some items you need to create a compost pile. Label the items, and answer the question.

1. Explain a decomposer's role in an ecosystem.

_____

_____

_____

Name: _____ **Date:** _____

Learning Content

Directions: Read the text, and answer the questions.

How Plants Create Food

Plants turn things that are not food—air, water, and sunlight—into food that they use to grow. This process is called photosynthesis. For this, plants need water, carbon dioxide from air, energy from sunlight, and chlorophyll. Chlorophyll is what makes plants green. It traps light energy from the sun so that it can be combined with carbon dioxide and water.

Plants don't always need all the food they make. They store this excess food in various parts of the plant, such as the stems, fruit, or roots. This food is stored in the form of glucose, which is a type of sugar. When people or animals eat these parts of the plant, they are able to use the stored energy.

1. What process do plants use to create food?

   a. sunlight

   b. photosynthesis

   c. growth

   d. chlorophyll

2. What makes plants green?

   a. chlorophyll

   b. stems

   c. photosynthesis

   d. carbon dioxide

3. Where is one place plants store extra food?

   a. soil

   b. air

   c. water

   d. stem

Name: _____ **Date:** _____

Directions: Study the diagram, and answer the questions.

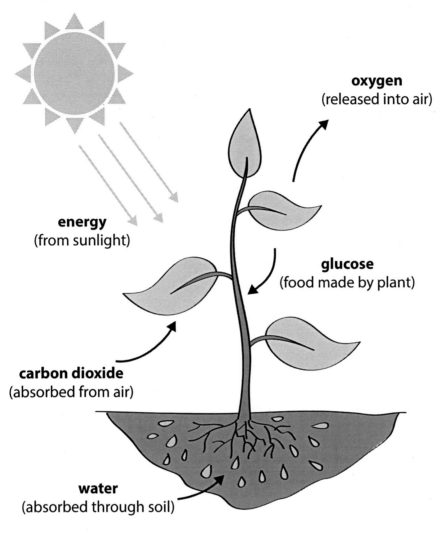

oxygen
(released into air)

energy
(from sunlight)

glucose
(food made by plant)

carbon dioxide
(absorbed from air)

water
(absorbed through soil)

1. What does the plant use to make food?

   a. oxygen, soil, and leaves   b. glucose, water, and soil

   c. soil, sunlight, and glucose   d. sunlight, carbon dioxide, and water

2. Where does the carbon dioxide come from?

   a. air   b. water

   c. sun   d. soil

3. What does the plant make for its food?

   a. oxygen   b. water

   c. glucose   d. carbon dioxide

Developing Questions

Name: _____   **Date:** _____

Directions: Read the text, and answer the questions.

Jeff buys three potted plants. It is a type of plant that needs lots of bright sunlight. He places one in a sunny window where it gets light for most of the day. He puts another where it gets light for a short time each day. The third goes in a room where it gets no sunlight at all. They each get half a cup of water every two days. Jeff wants to know how the amount of light the plants receive will affect photosynthesis.

Plant A:
Full Sun

Plant B:
Partial Sun

Plant C:
No Sun

1. Which plant will grow the most?

   a. Plant A

   b. Plant B

   c. Plant C

   d. They will all grow the same amount.

2. Which plant is most likely to die?

   a. Plant A

   b. Plant B

   c. Plant C

   d. They are equally likely to die.

3. What is a question you have about how sunlight affects the plants?

   _____

   _____

   _____

   _____

Name: _____ **Date:** _____

Directions: Read the text, and answer the questions.

Jeff has three potted plants. He places one in a sunny window where it gets light for most of the day. He puts another where it gets light for a short time each day. The third goes in a room where it gets no sunlight at all. They each get half a cup of water every two days. After two weeks, the plant with the most sun grew the most. The plant with some sun grew a little, and the plant with no sun is brown and wilted.

Plant A:
Full Sun

Plant B:
Partial Sun

Plant C:
No Sun

Planning Solutions

1. Which plant did not have what it needed for photosynthesis?

   a. Plant A

   b. Plant B

   c. Plant C

   d. They all had what they needed.

2. Why did Plant A grow the most?

   a. It made the most food.

   b. It made the least food.

   c. It had the most water.

   d. It had the most air.

3. How could Jeff create another experiment to test another element of photosynthesis?

   _____

   _____

   _____

Name: _____ **Date:** _____

Directions: Use the words in the box to label the diagram.

carbon dioxide	water	oxygen
energy	glucose	

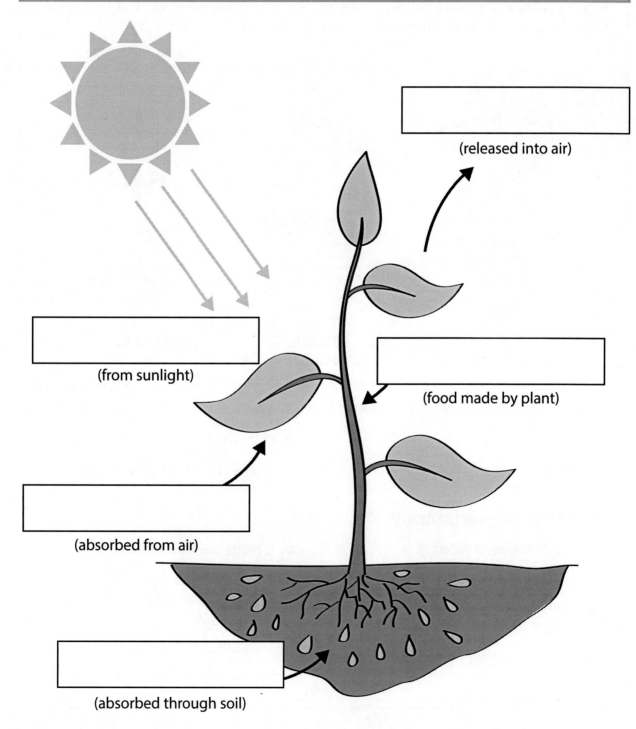

(released into air)

(from sunlight)

(food made by plant)

(absorbed from air)

(absorbed through soil)

Name: _____ **Date:** _____

Directions: Read the text, and answer the questions.

Building Your Own Healthy Ecosystem

An ecosystem is all the living and non-living things in an area. The living things need water, air, and minerals. They all need sunlight for energy. They need producers, or plants, to provide food for the consumers. They also need decomposers to recycle nutrients after plants and animals die.

Ecosystems need a stable climate. This allows plants to grow. It allows animals to reproduce. All things in an ecosystem depend on each other. Even small changes can cause harm. Ponds, oceans, and forests are all types of ecosystems.

Learning Content

1. What are non-living things that an ecosystem needs?

    a. plants, animals, and bacteria

    b. water, air, and plants

    c. water, air, and minerals

    d. plants, animals, and water

2. What are living things an ecosystem needs?

    a. producers, consumers, and minerals

    b. producers, consumers, and decomposers

    c. minerals, producers, and water

    d. water, air, and decomposers

3. Why do ecosystems need a stable climate?

    _____

    _____

Analyzing Data

Name: _____ Date: _____

Directions: Read the text, and study the chart. Then, answer the questions.

> Ponds are ecosystems. They have many living and nonliving things. The living things rely on everything in the ecosystem. Energy moves through the ecosystem from the sun to the plants to the animals.

	What It Needs
Duck	air, water to drink and find food, sunlight
Lilly pad	air, water, sunlight, nutrients
Cattails	air, water, sunlight, nutrients
Frog	air, water, sunlight, insects to eat
Grass	air, water, sunlight, nutrients
Worm	air, water, sunlight, decaying organisms for food
Grasshoppers	air, water, sunlight, plants to eat

1. Which nonliving thing gives the duck a place to find food?

   a. rock   **b.** water

   c. frog   **d.** grass

2. Which living thing returns nutrients to the ecosystem when plants and animals die?

   a. soil   **b.** frog

   c. duck   **d.** worm

3. What would happen to the animals if the plants disappeared? Why?

_____

_____

_____

_____

_____

Name: _____ Date: _____

Directions: Read the text, and answer the questions.

Henry wants to create an ecosystem in a fish tank. Underwater ecosystems usually include sand, rocks, plants, and different animals. With help from his older sister, he adds gravel to the bottom of the tank. Then he adds water and fish to the tank.

1. Which of these would make sense to add to the tank?

   a. snails

   b. plants

   c. sand

   d. all of the above

2. Will the fish tank ecosystem be exactly like an ecosystem in nature?

   a. No, but it will be similar.

   b. Yes, it will be exactly alike.

   c. No, it will be nothing alike.

   d. Yes, as long as he adds plants.

3. What is a question you have about creating a fish tank ecosystem?

   _____

   _____

Life Science

Planning Solutions

Name: _____ **Date:** _____

Directions: Read the text, and answer the questions.

> Henry created a fish tank ecosystem with the help of his older sister. He added gravel, sand, plants, different types of fish, snails, and small turtles. He didn't use anything to control temperature of the fish tank. One day, some of the plants in the tank were dead. A few days later, one of his fish was dead.

1. Why might the plants have died?

   a. The temperature was wrong.   **b.** The temperature was right.

   c. The fish did not get fed.   **d.** The turtles did not get fed.

2. If the temperature did not kill the fish, could the plants dying have affected the ecosystem? Why or why not?

   _____

   _____

3. How could Henry try to balance the ecosystem?

   _____

   _____

   _____

Name: _____ Date: _____

Communicating Results

Directions: Draw some animals to complete the ecosystem. Then, answer the question.

1. What animals did you draw?

_____

_____

_____

_____

2. Why did you choose these animals for this ecosystem?

_____

_____

3. What is a change that could harm this ecosystem?

_____

_____

Name: _____ Date: _____

Learning Content

Directions: Read the text, and answer the questions.

Can Matter Disappear?

We rely on our sense of sight a lot when we explore the world. However, there are many things that we can't see with our eyes. Matter is made of particles that are too small to be seen without magnification. Microscopes and other tools can magnify these particles so that we can study them. Even if we don't have a microscope, there are other ways we can study things we can't see. Have you ever tasted salt water? Even though you can't see the salt, you can taste it, so you know it's there.

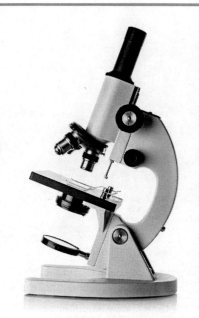

1. What is matter made of?

   a. large particles

   b. a few particles

   c. particles too small to see

   d. small particles you can see

2. What is a tool that can help you see particles?

   a. glasses

   b. microscope

   c. binoculars

   d. sunglasses

3. Do things exist that we cannot see?

   a. Yes, some things are too small to see.

   b. Yes, some things are too big to see.

   c. No, things disappear if we look away.

   d. No, only things that we can see exist.

51411—180 Days of Science

Name: _____ Date: _____

Directions: Read the text, and study the pictures. Then, answer the questions.

By looking at a glass of water, you can't tell that there is salt dissolved in it. When the water evaporates, the salt remains.

salt   water   salt water   water evaporates

Analyzing Data

1. Why can't you see the salt in the salt water?

   a. It disappears.

   b. It dissolves.

   c. It evaporates.

   d. It changes colors.

2. When the water evaporates, can you see the water anymore?

   a. Yes, you can see it floating in the air.

   b. Yes, but only if you add food coloring first.

   c. No, the particles of water are too small to see in the air.

   d. No, because water is clear.

3. Do you think the water still exists after it evaporates? Why or why not?

   _____

   _____

   _____

   _____

Developing Questions

Name: _____ **Date:** _____

Directions: Read the text, and answer the questions.

> Aaron has two bottles of water that look identical. One is salt water, and one is fresh water. Both bottles of water look clear. He wants to know which is which.

1. What can he do to find out which bottle has the salt water?

    a. Weigh them.

    b. Look at them.

    c. Listen to them.

    d. Touch them.

2. What is another way that Aaron could find out which bottle has salt water?

    a. He could let the water evaporate.

    b. He could put food coloring in the water.

    c. He could pour the water in the sink.

    d. He could mix the two bottles of water together.

3. What is a question Aaron might ask about properties of the salt water?

    _____

    _____

    _____

4. Do you think you could ever add so much salt to water that it wouldn't dissolve? Why or why not?

    _____

    _____

Name: _____ **Date:** _____

Directions: Read the text, and answer the questions.

> Things can float in salt water easier than they can in fresh water. This is because salt water is denser.
>
> Aaron has two cups of water. One is salt water, and one is fresh water. Both cups of water look clear. He wants to know which is which. He cannot taste the water.

1. An egg will sink in fresh water. What might happen if Aaron puts it in the salt water?

   a. It will float.   **b.** It will bounce.

   c. It will break.   **d.** It will turn blue.

2. If both cups have the same amount of water, and one has salt added, will they weigh the same?

   a. Yes, the weight of the salt disappears.

   b. Yes, because the salt absorbs some water.

   c. No, the total weight is combined, and the cup with salt will weigh more.

   d. No, the weight of the salt will be subtracted from the weight of the water.

3. Create a plan for Aaron to figure out what sinks in fresh water and floats in salt water.

   _____

   _____

   _____

4. What do you think would happen if Aaron boiled the water?

   _____

   _____

   _____

   _____

Communicating Results

Name: _____ Date: _____

Directions: Study the pictures, and answer the questions.

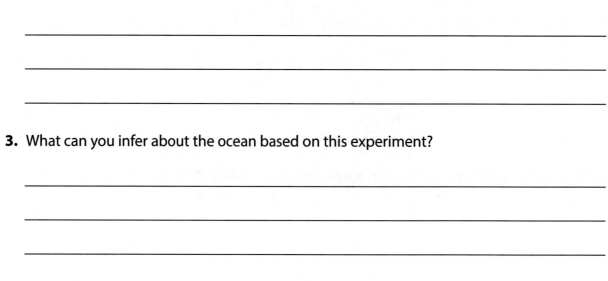

Fresh Water   Small Amount of Salt   Large Amount of Salt

1. How could you make the egg in the fresh water float?

   _____

   _____

   _____

2. How does the amount of salt in the water relate to how much the egg floats?

   _____

   _____

   _____

3. What can you infer about the ocean based on this experiment?

   _____

   _____

   _____

   _____

Name: _____ **Date:** _____

Directions: Read the text, and answer the questions.

How Do We Know Air Is There?

Matter is anything that has mass and takes up space. Air is matter. It is a mixture of gasses that move around us all the time, but it is also made of particles that are too small to be seen with our eyes.

Even though we can't see air, there are many ways we know it's there. We can breathe it in and blow it out. One of the ways we know air is there is by inflating a basketball. When it inflates with air, it changes shape and floats in water. Since air has mass, you can also weigh something before and after filling it with air. You will see that the weight increases.

1. What are the properties of matter?

   a. has mass and takes up space

   b. takes up space and has no mass

   c. has mass and does not take up space

   d. takes up space and is too small to see

2. Air is made of _____ that are _____ .

   a. particles, too big to see

   b. gases, too big to see

   c. particles, too small to see

   d. balloons, too small to see

3. What can you do to see if a balloon has air inside it?

   _____

   _____

   _____

Name: _____ **Date:** _____

Directions: Air takes up space even though you can't see it. The chart shows the circumference of a balloon as it is inflated. Look at the chart, and answer the questions.

Analyzing Data

Breaths	Circumference of Balloon (cm)
0	8
1	10
2	12
3	15
4	18
5	20
10	24

1. As air is added to the balloon, what happens?

    a. It gets larger.

    b. It gets smaller.

    c. It gets softer.

    d. It gets colder.

2. What is the air doing inside the balloon?

    a. Taking up space.

    b. Making the balloon heavier.

    c. Stretching the balloon.

    d. all of the above

3. What is another way that you could study the air inside the balloon?

    _____

    _____

    _____

    _____

    _____

Name: _____ **Date:** _____

Directions: Read the text, and answer the questions.

> Mia is going to mail her friend a present. She is sending her a fragile figurine. She wants to figure out the best way to pack the box.

1. If Mia puts the figurine in an empty box, what else is taking up space in the box?

   a. water   **b.** air

   c. electricity   **d.** energy

2. Which packing material uses air to protect fragile items?

   a. paper   **b.** bubble wrap

   c. ice packs   **d.** tissue paper

3. What is a question Mia could ask about different ways to pack the box?

_____

_____

_____

_____

Planning Solutions

Name: _____ Date: _____

Directions: Read the text, and answer the questions.

> Mia is going to mail her friend a present. She is sending her a fragile figurine packed in a box. She wants to figure out which material is best for wrapping the figurine. She has bubble wrap, tissue paper, and cloth.

1. When Mia adds packing material to the box, what happens to the amount of air in the box?

    a. It increases because there is air in all of the packing materials.

    b. It is completely removed from the box.

    c. It decreases because it is replaced with the packing materials.

    d. It stays the same.

2. Bubble wrap has a similar function to which object?

    a. air bag

    b. fan

    c. basketball

    d. horn

3. How can Mia conduct an experiment to find the best packing material?

    _____

    _____

    _____

4. How else can you use air to protect the figurine?

    _____

    _____

Name: _____ **Date:** _____

Directions: Design a model of a product that uses air as part of its function. For example, pool floats use air to help people float. You can make your own product or redesign one that already exists. Then, answer the questions.

1. What is your product?

   _____

   _____

   _____

2. Who would use your product, and how would they use it?

   _____

   _____

   _____

Learning Content

Name: _____ **Date:** _____

Directions: Read the text, and answer the questions.

How Air Moves Things

Air is all around us. We can't see air, but there are many ways to know it's there. We often notice air when it is moving. Moving air is called *wind*. We can feel the wind when it blows, and we can see it push objects. We can also see air when we blow bubbles under water.

Air has mass and takes up space. It is made of gasses that have particles too small for us to see. Even though we can't see air, it can be very powerful.

Moving air can push many different things. It can move large and small objects, depending on how hard it is blowing. For example, a gentle breeze might be able to blow a leaf, but a powerful gust of wind can rip off the roof of a building. Humans can use moving air for specific tasks, like generating electricity, sailing a boat, or flying a kite.

1. What can air do?

   a. inflate objects

   b. move objects

   c. make bubbles

   d. all of the above

2. Could air move a tree?

   a. Yes, a strong gust could move a tree.

   b. Yes, a gentle breeze could move a tree.

   c. No, trees are too strong to be moved by air.

   d. No, air is too weak to move a tree.

3. How could you move a ping pong ball without touching it?

   _____

   _____

51411—180 Days of Science   © *Shell Education*

Name: _____ **Date:** _____

Directions: The chart shows how far different objects move when someone blows on them with equal force. Look at the chart, and answer the questions.

Object	Distance Traveled (cm)
bottle cap	90
leaf	120
tissue	180
paper clip	110
block	0
marble	50

Analyzing Data

1. What do you think affects how far the object moves?

   a. the hardness of the object

   b. the weight of the object

   c. the color of the object

   d. the temperature of the object

2. If you blow harder on the paper clip, what would change?

   a. It wouldn't move as far.

   b. It would move farther.

   c. It would move backward.

   d. It wouldn't move at all.

3. You want to make sure that the force of the air is always exactly the same. What could you use to blow the objects besides your breath? Explain how this keeps the force the same.

   _____

   _____

   _____

   _____

Name: _____ Date: _____

Developing Questions

Directions: Read the text, and answer the questions.

> Asaf wants to build a balloon rocket. He attaches a straw to a balloon with tape and threads string through the straw. He attaches the string between two chairs set 3 meters (3.28 yards) apart. Asaf blows up the balloon a little bit and then lets it go. It travels 1 meter (1.09 yards).
>
>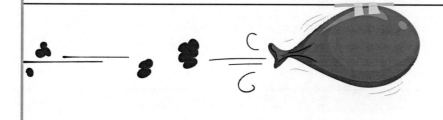

1. What moves the balloon rocket?

   a. water

   b. air

   c. electricity

   d. chemicals

2. What would make the balloon rocket go farther?

   a. inflating the balloon more

   b. inflating the balloon less

   c. not inflating the balloon

   d. filling the balloon with water

3. What is a question Asaf could ask about improving the balloon rocket?

   _____

   _____

   _____

   _____

   _____

 51411—180 Days of Science

Name: _____ **Date:** _____

Directions: Read the text, and answer the questions.

Asaf built a balloon rocket. He attached a straw to a balloon and threaded string through the straw. He attached the string between two chairs set 3 meters (3.28 yards) apart. When Asaf blew up the balloon a little bit and let it go, it only traveled 1 meter (1.09 yards) Asaf wants it to travel the whole length of the string.

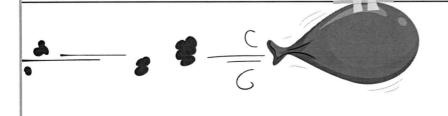

1. What could Asaf change about his rocket?

   a. amount of air in the balloon

   b. size of the balloon

   c. shape of the balloon

   d. any of these

2. What change could Asaf make to the string to make the rocket go farther?

   a. He could make the string higher where the rocket starts.

   b. He could make the string lower where the rocket starts.

   c. He could make the string loose so it hangs down.

   d. He could use a thick rope instead of string.

3. Plan another way for Asaf to use air to move something.

   _____

   _____

   _____

   _____

   _____

Planning Solutions

Communicating Results

Name: _____ **Date:** _____

Directions: Read the text, and study the chart. Title the graph, and graph the information from the chart. Then, answer the question.

> Asaf is using a straw to blow air on various objects. He blows with the same amount of force each time. He measures how far each object goes.

Object	Distance Traveled (cm)
bottle cap	90
leaf	120
tissue	180
paper clip	110
block	0
marble	50

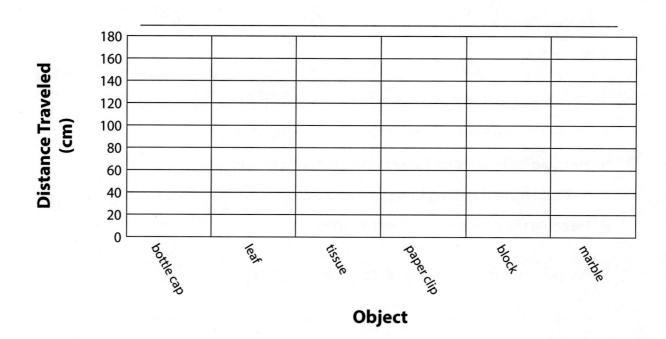

1. Why can't Asaf move the block when he blows on it?

_____

_____

_____

Name: _____ **Date:** _____

Learning Content

Directions: Read the text, and answer the questions.

Dissolving Sugar

Matter cannot be created or destroyed. This means that when you combine two types of matter, the combined mass of the matter stays the same. You can rearrange objects in different ways, but the mass will never change. This even applies when you can no longer see the matter. For example, if you dissolve 28 g of sugar in 230 g of water, the weight of the mixture will be 258 grams. You will not be able to see the sugar in the water, but the amount of combined matter stays the same.

1. How does the amount of matter change when you mix two types of matter?

   a. It stays the same.   **b.** It doubles.

   c. It triples.   **d.** It is cut in half.

2. What is one way you can tell that the sugar is still in the water after it dissolves?

   a. Weigh the mixture.   **b.** Look at the mixture.

   c. Touch the mixture.   **d.** Listen to the mixture.

3. If you only added 20 g of sugar to 230 g of water, how much would the mixture weigh?

   a. 250 g   **b.** 240 g

   c. 260 g   **d.** 230 g

4. Why do you think you can't see the sugar when it's mixed with water?

   _____

   _____

   _____

Name: _____ **Date:** _____

Analyzing Data

Directions: When you combine matter, the total weight of matter stays the same. Look at the chart, and answer the questions.

Sugar (g)	Water (g)	Total Weight (g)
25	7	32
7	25	32
100	100	200
2	100	102

1. The total weight _____ the combined weight of the sugar and water.

   a. sometimes equals

   b. usually equals

   c. never equals

   d. always equals

2. If you add 50 additional grams of sugar to 200 g of sugar water, what will the new mixture weigh?

   a. 200 g

   b. 250 g

   c. 50 g

   d. 150 g

3. If you boil the sugar water in an enclosed area and retain all the water that evaporates, how will the total weight change?

   _____

   _____

   _____

   _____

51411—180 Days of Science

Name: _____ **Date:** _____

Directions: Read the text, and answer the questions.

Ben is going to bake cookies. He uses a food scale to measure his ingredients. He needs 131 g of sugar, 113 g of butter, and 241 g of flour. He adds all the ingredients to a bowl.

NET WT 5 LB (2.26 kg)   NET WT. 4 LBS. (1.81kg)

1. When Ben combines the ingredients, how much will the mixture weigh?

    a. 450 g   **b.** 485 g

    c. 500 g   **d.** 400 g

2. If he adds 340 g of chocolate chips to the mixture, how much will it weigh?

    a. 825 g   **b.** 790 g

    c. 840 g   **d.** 740 g

3. What happens if Ben scoops some batter out of the bowl?

    a. The batter in the bowl will weigh less.   **b.** The batter in the bowl will weigh more.

    c. The weight of the batter in the bowl will stay the same.   **d.** The batter in the bowl will increase.

4. What is a question Ben can ask about the weight of the combined ingredients?

    _____

    _____

5. Describe how the combined weight of the batter will be affected when you scoop the dough onto a pan?

    _____

    _____

Developing Questions

Name: _____ Date: _____

Directions: Read the text, and answer the questions.

Darla and her mom are making vegetable soup for dinner. Darla weighs the pot. It weighs 2.5 kg. They add 450 g of carrots, 900 g of water, and 225 g of celery. Darla wants to know how much the mixture of food weighs.

1. How can Darla weigh just the food once it's in the pot?

   a. Add the weight of the food and the weight of the pot.

   b. Subtract the weight of the pot from the total weight.

   c. Subtract the weight of the carrots from the total weight.

   d. Subtract the weight of the celery from the total weight.

2. If they cook the soup with the lid on, what will the total weight of the soup be once it's cooked? Do not include the weight of the pot.

   a. 2,000 g

   b. 4,080 g

   c. 1,000 g

   d. 1,575 g

3. If they cook the soup with the lid off, some of the water will evaporate. How can Darla tell how much water has evaporated once the soup is cooked?

   _____

   _____

   _____

   _____

Name: _____ **Date:** _____

Directions: Read the text, and study the data. Complete the Total Lemonade column. Then, title the graph, and graph the data from the Total Lemonade column.

Lemonade is made using sugar, water, and lemon juice. You can increase the servings by increasing the ingredients.

Amount of Sugar (cups)	Amount of Water (cups)	Amount of Lemon Juice (cups)	Total Lemonade (cups)
1	4	1	
2	8	2	
3	12	3	
4	16	4	

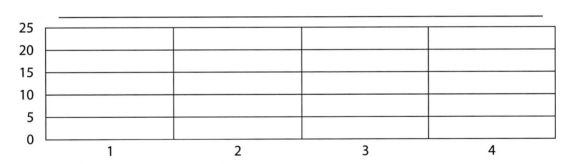

1. If you keep the ratio of ingredients the same, will the lemonade taste the same when you make more servings? Why or why not?

_____

_____

_____

_____

Communicating Results

Learning Content

Name: _____ **Date:** _____

Directions: Read the text, and answer the questions.

Ice and Water

You probably know that you can freeze water to make ice. You can boil water to create water vapor. Matter, like water, can also be a solid, a liquid, or a gas. When matter changes from one state to another, the total weight stays the same. This is true even if the matter looks like it disappeared.

Matter may have a different volume in different states. This means that it will take up a different amount of space. The weight will not change. If you freeze a bowl of water, it will weigh the same before and after it is frozen, but the frozen water will have a greater volume. If you let ice melt, it will still weigh the same, but the volume will decrease. If you boil water, the weight of the water vapor will not change even though the water seems to disappear.

1. When water changes from liquid to solid, how is the amount of matter affected?

   a. It stays the same.

   b. It doubles.

   c. It triples.

   d. It is cut in half.

2. When water freezes, it takes up _____ .

   a. less space

   b. the same amount of space

   c. more space

   d. half the space

3. When you boil water, the water vapor seems to disappear. Which property tells you that none of it disappears?

   a. texture

   b. smell

   c. color

   d. weight

Name: _____ **Date:** _____

Directions: When matter changes states, its weight does not change. Study the picture, and answer the questions.

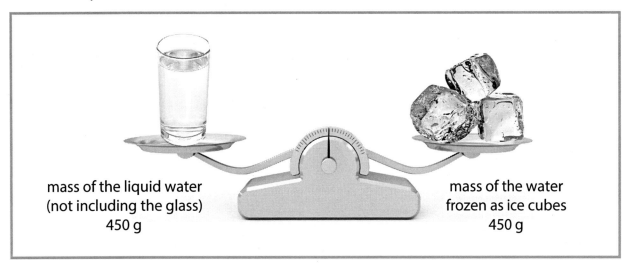

mass of the liquid water
(not including the glass)
450 g

mass of the water
frozen as ice cubes
450 g

Analyzing Data

1. What is the weight of the liquid water?

   a. 450 g

   b. 900 g

   c. 400 g

   d. 475 g

2. What is the weight of the water after it freezes?

   a. 900 g

   b. 225 g

   c. 450 g

   d. 475 g

3. If you melt the ice, what will happen to the weight?

   _____

   _____

   _____

   _____

Name: _____ **Date:** _____

Directions: Read the text, and answer the questions.

Sean is making chocolate candies with his mom for his brother's birthday. They have 225 g of chocolate. They melt the chocolate and place it into heart-shaped candy molds. Then, they put the chocolate in the freezer to harden.

1. How can Sean test to see if any chocolate disappears when he melts it and freezes it?

   a. Weigh it when it is melted.

   b. Weigh it when it is melted and frozen.

   c. Weigh it before they melt it and after they melt it.

   d. Weigh it when it is frozen.

2. Will freezing the chocolate in small pieces instead of one large piece change the total weight?

   a. Yes, the total weight will be less.

   b. Yes, the total weight will be more.

   c. No, the total weight will be the same.

   d. No, but the shape of the mold could change it.

3. What is a question Sean can ask about the different states of matter?

   _____

   _____

   _____

   _____

Name: _____ **Date:** _____

Directions: Read the text, and answer the questions.

Carla and her family are going camping. They decide to bring two coolers with them. One cooler has 36 lbs. of ice cubes, and the other cooler has 24 lbs. of ice cubes. Carla is not sure if the coolers will be the same weight as they started when the ice melts.

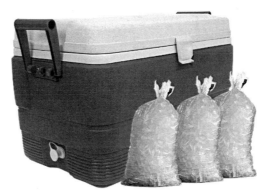

Planning Solutions

1. The ice fills the coolers to the top because there is a lot of space between the cubes. What will happen when the ice melts?

   a. The water take up more space and overflow.

   b. The water will take up less space than the ice.

   c. The water will disappear when the ice melts.

   d. The water will take up the same amount of space.

2. Would a solid block of ice take up a different amount of space than ice cubes?

   a. Yes, because ice cubes have air between them, and a solid block doesn't.

   b. Yes, because ice cubes expand more than a solid block of ice.

   c. No, they take up the same amount of space.

   d. No, it is impossible to create a solid block of ice.

3. How can Carla create an experiment with the two coolers to prove that the weight of ice is the same as the melted ice?

   _____

   _____

   _____

Name: _____ **Date:** _____

Directions: Study the chart. Then, answer the questions.

Volume of Water (mL)	Volume of Ice (mL)
10	10.9
20	21.8
30	32.7
40	43.6

Amount of Water (grams)	Amount of Ice (grams)
250	250
500	500
750	750
1000	1000

1. Describe what happens to the volume of water when you freeze it.

_____

_____

_____

2. Describe what happens to the amount of water when you freeze it.

_____

_____

_____

3. Suppose you weigh ice and weigh it again once it melts. If the weights do not match, what do you think happened?

_____

_____

_____

4. How would adding salt to water before you freeze it affect the weight?

_____

_____

_____

Name: _____ **Date:** _____

Directions: Read the text. Answer the questions.

Powders and Minerals

Sugar and salt look alike. Baking powder and baking soda look alike, too. Things may look the same, but there are ways to find out what they are. You can find out what they are by looking at their properties. There are physical and chemical properties. Examples of physical properties are color and mass. Reactions to other substances would show chemical properties.

Learning Content

1. What can we use to identify materials?

   a. salt
   b. baking soda
   c. properties
   d. substances

2. What is an example of a chemical property?

   a. color
   b. reaction to other substances
   c. mass
   d. melting point

3. If you added vinegar to a substance to see the reaction, what type of property are you testing?

   a. chemical
   b. physical
   c. color
   d. hardness

4. Do you think you have to change a substance to test physical properties? Why or why not?

   _____

   _____

Analyzing Data

Name: _____ **Date:** _____

Directions: Read the text, and look at the chart. Then, answer the questions.

You can identify some materials based on their reactions to water, vinegar, and iodine.

	Color	Reaction to Water	Reaction to Vinegar	Reaction to Iodine
Baking Soda	white	none	lots of bubbling	none
Sugar	white	none	none	none
Salt	white	none	none	none
Cornstarch	white	none	none	blue-black
Baking Powder	white	bubbling	bubbling	bubbling, blue-black

1. If a substance reacts to vinegar with lots of bubbling, what is it?

   a. baking powder

   b. cornstarch

   c. baking soda

   d. sugar

2. If a substance turns blue-black when it reacts to iodine and does not bubble, what is it?

   a. cornstarch

   b. baking powder

   c. baking soda

   d. sugar

3. Which substance bubbles with water?

   a. sugar

   b. salt

   c. baking powder

   d. baking soda

4. If a substance turns blue-black when iodine is added to it, what else should you look at to determine what it is?

   _____

   _____

Name: _____ **Date:** _____

Directions: Read the text, and answer the questions.

Kirk is going to help his mom bake. He has three unlabeled containers of white powder. He wants to find out what they are.

1. What can Kirk examine that will not change the powders in any way?

    a. granule size

    b. reaction to water

    c. reaction to vinegar

    d. reaction to iodine

2. Kirk decides the powders look the same. What is another property he could examine?

    a. smell

    b. texture

    c. hardness

    d. all of the above

3. What is a question Kirk can ask to learn more about the powders?

    _____

    _____

    _____

4. Just because the powders are all white, does that mean they will all work the same way in a recipe? Why or why not?

    _____

    _____

Name: _____ **Date:** _____

Directions: Read the text, and answer the questions.

> Kirk is going to help his mom bake. He has three unlabeled containers of white powder. He wants to find out what they are. He does not want to taste them. He has water, vinegar, and iodine on hand.

1. Kirk puts some of the first powder in a bowl for testing. How can he make sure the reaction he tests is the result of only one combination?

   a. mix just one of the liquids with the powder

   b. mix the water and iodine with the powder

   c. mix the water and vinegar with the powder

   d. mix all of the liquids with the powder

2. Why is it important to test one combination at a time?

   a. So you know how much the combination weighs.

   b. So you can use a small container.

   c. So you know what is causing the reaction.

   d. It is not important.

3. Explain how Kirk can use what he has to determine what the three powders are.

   _____

   _____

   _____

4. Do you think putting two liquids into one powder would help Kirk figure out what the powder is? Why or why not?

   _____

   _____

   _____

Planning Solutions

Name: _____ Date: _____

Directions: Read Kirk's notes. Complete the chart, and answer the questions.

> I know I have baking soda, powdered sugar, and cornstarch. I don't know which one is which. Powder A bubbled with vinegar and had no other reactions. Powder B turned blue-black with iodine and had no other reactions. Powder C had no reactions.
>
> From my research, I know that cornstarch changes color when mixed with iodine. Baking soda bubbles with vinegar. Baking powder bubbles with everything.

	Color	Reaction to Water	Reaction to Vinegar	Reaction to Iodine
Powder A	white			
Powder B	white			
Powder C	white			

1. What do you think each of the powders are? Why?

_____

_____

_____

2. What is a white powder that would have bubbled with water, vinegar, and iodine?

_____

3. Is Kirk testing physical or chemical properties? Briefly explain what chemical and physical properties are.

_____

_____

_____

_____

_____

Communicating Results

Name: _____ **Date:** _____

Directions: Read the text, and answer the questions.

Metals

We use many metals in our everyday lives. We have metal utensils, cans, cars, and zippers. Not all metals are alike, though. We can tell a lot about different metals by observing their properties. Some metals are magnetic. This means that they are attracted to magnets. Metals are usually shiny. Some metals are very hard, and some are softer. Some metals are good conductors of heat or electricity, and some are not as good. Depending on their properties, different metals are good for different things.

There are many types of metals. Some are pure metals, such as iron and gold. Many metals that we use are alloys. Alloys are metals that are combined with other elements. Steel is an alloy that is very strong. Steel is iron combined with carbon. You may have heard of stainless steel, which is used in many kitchen appliances. This is steel mixed with an element called *chromium*.

1. What is an example of a metal object?
   a. ball
   b. sofa
   c. can
   d. television

2. What does metal look like?
   a. shiny
   b. wood
   c. plastic
   d. soft

3. Many metals _____ heat and electricity well.
   a. stop
   b. conduct
   c. listen to
   d. feel

4. What is steel?
   a. aluminum mixed with carbon
   b. iron mixed with carbon
   c. iron mixed with stainless steel
   d. stainless steel mixed with alloys

5. What are two metal things you use in your daily life?

   _____

   _____

Name: _____ **Date:** _____

Directions: You can identify metals based on their properties. Read the text, and study the chart. Then, answer the questions.

Analyzing Data

Metal	Properties	What It's Good For
gold	shiny, nonmagnetic, doesn't corrode, good conductor of electricity and heat, soft, flexible	jewelry, coins
silver	shiny, nonmagnetic, good conductor of electricity, soft	jewelry, coins, utensils, dentistry
iron	shiny, magnetic, corrodes (rusts), strong, hard	used to make steel, kitchen equipment
copper	shiny, nonmagnetic, resistant to corrosion, good conductor of electricity and heat, flexible	water pipes, electrical wire, decorative items
mercury	shiny, nonmagnetic, good conductor of electricity, liquid at room temperature	thermometers, light bulbs
aluminum	shiny, nonmagnetic, good conductor of electricity and heat, soft, flexible	cans, airplanes, foil

1. Why is gold good for jewelry?

   a. It doesn't corrode.   b. It is liquid at room temperature.

   c. It corrodes.   d. It is silver.

2. Which is liquid at room temperature?

   a. gold   b. iron

   c. silver   d. mercury

3. Which metal is magnetic?

   a. gold   b. aluminum

   c. iron   d. silver

Developing Questions

Name: _____ **Date:** _____

Directions: Read the text, and answer the questions.

Amy has three different types of metals. She wants to figure out what they are.

---

1. What is something Amy should examine about the metals?

   a. magnetism   **b.** taste

   c. size   **d.** sound

2. Amy could test _____ to see if the metal is attracted to magnets.

   a. magnetism   **b.** shine

   c. hardness   **d.** flexibility

3. What is a question Amy can ask to learn more about the metals?

   _____

   _____

   _____

4. Describe how the foil's properties are different from the pan's properties.

   _____

   _____

   _____

   _____

Name: _____   Date: _____

Directions: Read the text, and answer the questions.

Amy has metal foil, a coin, and a kitchen pan. She is examining their properties to figure out what kind of metal they are. She knows that iron rusts, aluminum is flexible, and gold doesn't rust.

1. If the foil bends easily, it is probably made of _____.

   a. gold

   b. iron

   c. aluminum

   d. mercury

2. Amy gets the pan wet, and in a few days, it has rust. It is probably made of _____.

   a. iron

   b. silver

   c. copper

   d. gold

3. What are some other tests that Amy could conduct on her metals?

   _____

   _____

   _____

4. If Amy has a piece of gold jewelry and a piece of silver jewelry, what is the easiest way for her to tell which is which?

   _____

Name: _____ **Date:** _____

Communicating Results

Directions: Read the text. Title the graph, and graph the hardness of the metals. Then, answer the question.

A metal's hardness can be measured using the Mohs' scale. A measurement of 1 is the softest. A measurement of 10 is the hardest.

Metal	Mohs' Scale Hardness
gold	2.5
silver	2.5
aluminum	2.5
steel	4

Metal	Mohs' Scale Hardness
copper	3
iron	4
titanium carbide	8.5
tungsten carbide	9

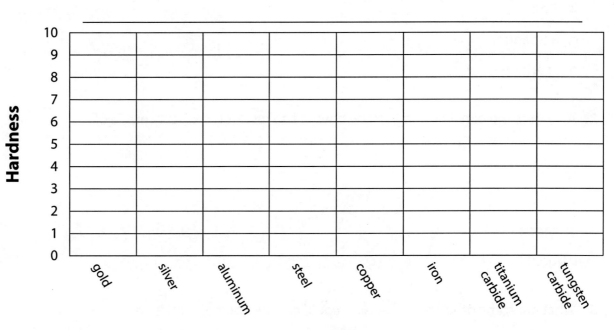

1. What do you think would be a good use for the harder metals?

_____

_____

_____

51411—180 Days of Science

Name: _____ **Date:** _____

Directions: Read the text, and answer the questions.

Mix It Up!

Mixing things can produce amazing reactions. New substances with different properties can be formed. Baking soda and vinegar are fun to mix. Baking soda is sodium bicarbonate. Vinegar contains acetic acid. When you mix them, you get a lot of fizz and bubbles. This is because new substances have formed. The new substances include liquids and gases. The gases cause all the bubbles.

Sometimes when you mix things, a physical change happens. Mixing salt and water is an example of a physical change. These changes affect the form of substances but not their composition. Physical changes can sometimes be reversed.

Sometimes mixing things causes chemical changes. Mixing baking soda and vinegar is a chemical change. Chemical changes create at least one new substance and often can't be reversed.

1. When you mix vinegar and baking soda, _____ are formed.

   a. sodium bicarbonate

   b. acetic acid

   c. old substances

   d. new substances

2. Where do the bubbles come from when you mix baking soda and vinegar?

   a. gas

   b. water

   c. physical changes

   d. metal

3. When you mix baking soda and vinegar, what kind of change happens?

   a. physical

   b. chemical

   c. reversible

   d. subtle

4. What is the difference between a physical change and a chemical change?

   _____

   _____

Analyzing Data

Name: _____ **Date:** _____

Directions: Read the text. Study the chart, and answer the questions.

You can blow up a balloon with baking soda and vinegar. Jeff is testing to see if using more baking soda will make the balloon inflate more. He tests each combination three times to make sure his results are reliable. Each trial has slightly different results. He will average his results for each amount of baking soda. Each trial in the chart used the same amount of vinegar.

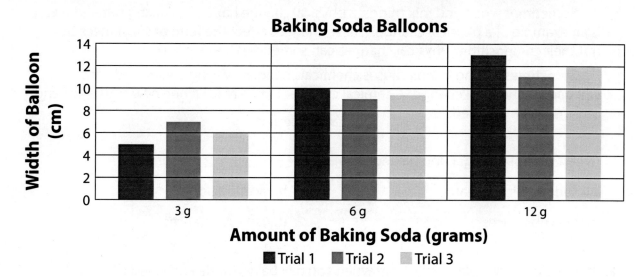

Baking Soda Balloons

Width of Balloon (cm)

Amount of Baking Soda (grams)

■ Trial 1   ■ Trial 2   ■ Trial 3

1. What happens when you increase the amount of baking soda?

   a. The balloon inflates less.   **b.** The balloon inflates more.

   c. The balloon stays the same.   **d.** The balloon doesn't inflate.

2. Doing multiple trials makes sure that the results are _____.

   a. reliable   **b.** wrong

   c. different   **d.** random

3. Which amount of baking soda creates the least amount of gas?

   a. 12 grams   **b.** 6 grams

   c. 3 grams   **d.** 24 grams

Name: _____ Date: _____

Directions: Read the text, and answer the questions.

> Reid wants to make a volcano for a science project. He wants it to look like it erupts, so he is using vinegar and baking soda. He tries 500 mL of vinegar and 4 grams of baking soda. The reaction is small. Then he tries 500 mL of vinegar and 5 grams of baking soda. The reaction is a little bigger. He knows he should just change one thing at a time about his experiment.

Developing Questions

1. What should Reid increase?

   a. vinegar   **b.** baking soda

   c. both a and b   **d.** water

2. When conducting investigations, how many things should you change each time?

   a. all of them   **b.** one

   c. all but one   **d.** two

3. What is a question Reid can ask about finding the best amount of vinegar and baking soda?

   _____

   _____

   _____

4. Do you think Reid should repeat the experiment more than once with the same measurements? Why or why not?

   _____

   _____

Planning Solutions

Name: _____ **Date:** _____

Directions: Read the text, and answer the questions.

Reid wants to make a volcano for a science project. He is using vinegar and baking soda for the "lava." He tries 500 mL of vinegar and 4 grams of baking soda one time. The reaction is small. Then he tries 500 mL of vinegar and 8 grams of baking soda one time. The reaction is bigger. He knows he should just change one thing at a time about his experiment. He also knows he should repeat each test more than once to make sure he's getting accurate results.

1. With just one trial of each test, will Reid be sure his results are accurate?

   a. Yes, doing them once is enough.

   b. Yes, there is no way he made a mistake.

   c. No, he should repeat them to be sure.

   d. No, the results of the first trial are always wrong.

2. Reid wants a larger reaction. What should he try?

   a. decreasing baking soda to 2 g

   b. increasing baking soda to 12 g

   c. increasing vinegar to 600 mL

   d. increasing vinegar to 700 mL

3. How should Reid plan his experiment so that his results are reliable?

   _____

   _____

   _____

4. What should Reid do to make sure he keeps track of all of his trials accurately?

   _____

   _____

   _____

   _____

Name: _____ **Date:** _____

Directions: Read the text. Title the graph, and graph the data from the chart. Then, answer the questions.

Stephanie was inflating a balloon with a mixture of vinegar and baking soda. She measured the width of the balloon after each trial. Each amount of baking soda was mixed with the same amount of vinegar. Her results are in the chart below.

Baking Soda (grams)	Trial 1 (centimeters)	Trial 2 (centimeters)	Trial 3 (centimeters)
4 g	7	6	8
8 g	10	12	11
14 g	15	13	13

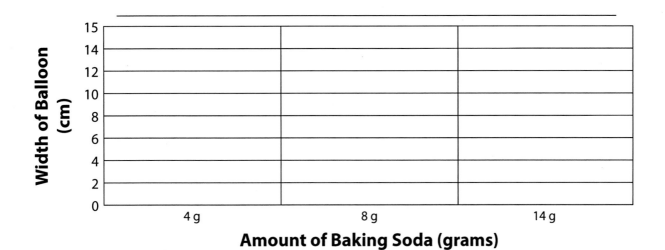

1. What amount of baking soda should you use for the biggest balloon?

   _____

2. How do you think reducing the vinegar would affect the results?

   _____

   _____

   _____

Communicating Results

Learning Content

Name: _____ Date: _____

Directions: Read the text, and answer the questions.

A Messy Mixture

You probably think of mixing dough as a way to make something yummy. It is more complex than that, though. When you mix ingredients, it can form a new substance that has different properties. This is called a chemical change. Chemical changes often cannot be reversed. For example, most bread recipes call for yeast. When yeast and sugar are mixed, the yeast eats the sugar. This produces new substances: carbon dioxide gas and ethanol. The carbon dioxide becomes trapped in the bread dough and creates many bubbles in the dough. This is how bread rises.

You can also mix other things that result in fun, new substances. Mixing water, glue, and borax makes slime. When you mix these things, the chemical change results in something new that you can play with.

1. When you mix yeast and sugar, _____ and ethanol are formed.

   a. sodium bicarbonate

   b. carbon dioxide

   c. carbon monoxide

   d. bread

2. What causes bread to rise?

   a. gas

   b. water

   c. acetic acid

   d. sugar

3. Does bread dough have the same properties as flour, water, and yeast separately? How do you know?

   _____

   _____

4. What kind of change happens when you mix glue and borax? How do you know?

   _____

   _____

51411—180 Days of Science

Name: _____ **Date:** _____

Directions: Read the text, and study the chart. Then, answer the questions.

Mixing some substances causes physical changes, which can sometimes be reversed. Some mixtures cause chemical changes. This results in new substances and often cannot be reversed. The chart below shows what happens when you mix two different substances.

Analyzing Data

Substance 1	Substance 2	Result	Chemical or Physical Change
water	sand	wet sand	physical
vinegar	baking soda	carbon dioxide	chemical
yeast	sugar	carbon dioxide	chemical
glue	borax	slime	chemical
flour	salt	flour and salt mixture	physical

1. Does mixing sand and water result in a chemical or physical change?

   a. chemical   **b.** physical

   c. neither   **d.** both a and b

2. Mixing yeast and sugar results in a _____ change.

   a. chemical   **b.** physical

   c. carbon dioxide   **d.** salt

3. Explain how you know that mixing vinegar and baking soda results in a chemical change.

_____

_____

Developing Questions

Name: _____ **Date:** _____

Directions: Read the text, and answer the questions.

Delilah wants to make homemade slime. She has glue, water, and borax. Her recipe calls for 120 mL water, 120 mL glue, and 1 teaspoon of borax.

1. Once Delilah mixes the slime, can she separate it into separate parts again?

   a. Yes, it was a physical change, and physical changes can always reversed.

   b. Yes, it was a chemical change, and chemical changes can always be reversed.

   c. No, it was a physical change, and physical changes can't ever be reversed.

   d. No, it was a chemical change, and this chemical change can't be reversed.

2. Delilah only has 60 mL of glue and 60 mL of water. How much borax should she use?

   a. ¼ teaspoon

   b. ½ teaspoon

   c. ¾ teaspoon

   d. 2 teaspoons

3. What is a question Delilah can ask about the slime mixture?

   _____

   _____

   _____

4. How can you tell that the mixture results in a chemical change?

   _____

   _____

   _____

Planning Solutions

Name: _____ **Date:** _____

Directions: Read the text, and answer the questions.

Han is baking bread with his parents. They add yeast to the dough without measuring it properly. They decide to let the dough rise to see what happens.

1. If the dough does not rise much, that means there was _____ yeast.

    a. too much   **b.** not enough

    c. no   **d.** a lot of

2. If the dough rises twice as much as it should have, there was _____ yeast.

    a. no   **b.** not enough

    c. too much   **d.** inactive

3. How can Han and his parents create an experiment to find the right amount of yeast?

_____

_____

_____

_____

4. If you have a very dense piece of bread and a very fluffy piece of bread, which do you think has more yeast? Why?

_____

_____

Name: _____ **Date:** _____

Communicating Results

Directions: Draw a picture of at least two substances that create something new when mixed. Label your drawing, and answer the question.

1. Explain what you drew. What is created when you mix your two substances?

_____

_____

_____

Name: _____ **Date:** _____

Directions: Read the text, and answer the questions.

How the Sun Helps Feed Us

Food gives your body the energy it needs to grow, move, heal, and stay warm. Have you ever thought about where that energy comes from? The ultimate source of energy for all life on Earth is the sun. Energy from sunlight moves up through the food chain and sustains life on Earth. Plants use energy from sunlight for photosynthesis. This is how they make their food. In turn, plants are food for other animals. Without sunlight, there would be no plants, no animals, and no people.

1. What is the ultimate source of energy for all life on Earth?

   a. plants   **b.** water

   c. sunlight   **d.** bread

2. Through which process do plants make food?

   a. photosynthesis   **b.** photographs

   c. energy   **d.** heat

3. If there was no sun, what would live on Earth?

   a. humans   **b.** plants

   c. insects   **d.** nothing

4. If plants suddenly died, do you think energy could still be transferred from the sun to feed us? Why or why not?

   _____

   _____

   _____

Analyzing Data

Name: _____   Date: _____

Directions: Read the text, and study the chart. Then, answer the questions.

> Animals get energy from food. When they have more energy than they need, it is stored as fat. This makes an animal gain weight. If they don't have enough food, they use stored fat for energy. This makes an animal lose weight. Energy can be measured in units called the kilocalorie, or kcal. The chart below shows how many kcals each cat needs per day and how many kcals they get per week.

	Energy Needs Per Day (kcal)	Energy Acquired in One Week (kcal)	Too Much or Too Little?
Cat 1	200	1300	too little
Cat 2	300	2100	just right
Cat 3	250	2000	too much

1. Which cat would lose weight?

   a. Cat 3

   b. Cat 1

   c. Cat 2

   d. none of them

2. Which cat would stay the same weight?

   a. Cat 1

   b. Cat 3

   c. Cat 2

   d. none of them

3. What would happen if Cat 3 ate too much food for a long time? How do you know?

   _____

   _____

   _____

   _____

Name: _____ **Date:** _____

Directions: Read the text, and answer the questions.

> Jeff is a farmer. He grows cabbage and has chickens. Grasshoppers eat the cabbage, and chickens eat the grasshoppers. When the chickens are mature, Jeff sells them at the market.
>
>

1. Which organism uses energy from the sun to make food?

    a. grasshopper

    b. chicken

    c. cabbage

    d. humans

2. Which organisms can transfer energy to humans?

    a. cabbage and soil

    b. soil and chickens

    c. chickens

    d. chickens and cabbage

3. What could you ask about the amount of energy that transfers from the grasshoppers to the chickens?

    _____

    _____

    _____

Name: _____ **Date:** _____

Planning Solutions

Directions: Read the text, and answer the questions.

Anna is making a dinner of grilled chicken, rice, and salad for her family. She and her husband eat the whole meal. Their son eats only the chicken and rice. Their daughter eats only the rice and salad.

1. Which person's meal has energy from only plants?

   a. son

   b. daugher

   c. mother

   d. father

2. Where did the energy in the son's food come from?

   a. rice and salad

   b. chicken

   c. rice and chicken

   d. salad and rice

3. How can you create a meal that got all of its energy directly from the sun?

   _____

   _____

   _____

   _____

Name: _____ **Date:** _____

Directions: Draw a picture of how energy is transferred from the sun to humans in food. Label your drawing. Then, answer the question.

1. Describe how energy travels from the sun to make your favorite meal.

_____

_____

_____

Learning Content

Name: _____ **Date:** _____

Directions: Read the text, and answer the questions.

Energy Flow through Food Chains

All of the energy in our food came from the sun. Energy is passed from the sun through the food chain. Plants, also called *producers*, are the first level. They use sunlight for photosynthesis. This is how they make their own food. Animals that eat plants are the next level. They are also known as *primary consumers*. The third level is animals that eat plant-eating animals. These are *secondary consumers*. Only about 10 percent of the energy at any level of the food chain is transferred to the next level. The rest as lost is heat through metabolic processes. These are things like turning food into energy that the body can use.

1. How much energy is passed from one level of the food chain to the next?

   a. 100 percent   **b.** 10 percent

   c. 1 percent   **d.** 50 percent

2. Can animals use energy directly from the sun?

   a. Yes, animals make food through photosynthesis.   **b.** Yes, animals get energy when they lay in the sun.

   c. No, animals must eat plants or other animals for energy.   **d.** No, there are too many cloudy days for this.

3. Where do people get their energy from?

   _____

   _____

4. Why is some energy lost between levels of the food chain?

   _____

   _____

Name: _____ **Date:** _____

Directions: Read the text, and study the diagram. Then, answer the questions.

Energy is transferred from the sun throughout the food chain. There is a loss of energy at each level. The energy is lost mostly as heat.

Energy Flows through Food Chains

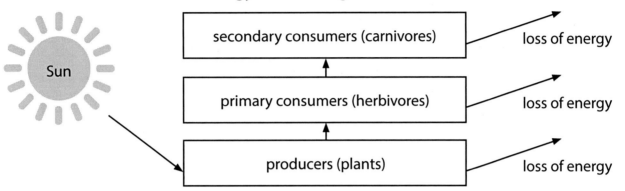

1. Does all of the energy from the producers transfer to the primary consumers?

   a. Yes, all of the energy is transferred.

   b. No, there is a loss of energy as heat.

   c. Yes, as long as the primary consumer eats the plant quickly.

   d. No, there is a loss of energy as sound.

2. Which organisms use energy directly from the sun?

   a. carnivores

   b. herbivores

   c. plants

   d. decomposers

3. Can secondary consumers use energy directly from the sun? Why or why not?

   _____

   _____

   _____

   _____

Analyzing Data

Name: _____   Date: _____

Directions: Read the text, and answer the questions.

In a simple food chain, clover uses sunlight for photosynthesis, a rabbit eats clover, a snake eats the rabbit, and an eagle eats the snake.

Developing Questions

1. Which organism gets energy directly from the sun?

   a. eagle

   b. snake

   c. clover

   d. rabbit

2. In this food chain, would the eagle survive if the rabbits died out?

   a. Yes, the eagle would get energy directly from the sun.

   b. No, because the sun's energy would stop with the clover.

   c. Yes, the eagle would eat clover instead.

   d. No, because the sun's energy would stop with the snakes.

3. What could Jennifer ask about the energy transfer from plant to animal?

   _____

   _____

   _____

   _____

Planning Solutions

Name: _____ **Date:** _____

Directions: Read the text, and answer the questions.

A kilocalorie (kcal) is a unit of energy. Matt's family serves dinner. If he eats chicken, he gets 146 kcal from 100 g of chicken breast. He gets 111 kcal from 100 g of brown rice. He gets 34 kcal from 100 g of broccoli, and he gets 406 kcal from 100 g of cheese.

1. Which food would give Matt the most energy?

   a. chicken

   b. brown rice

   c. cheese

   d. They are all the same.

2. Can Matt still eat enough if he chooses rice instead of chicken?

   a. Yes, the servings have similar amounts of energy.

   b. Yes, the rice has more energy than the chicken.

   c. No, the rice has much less energy than the chicken.

   d. No, the rice does not contain any energy.

3. How can Matt investigate how much energy comes from other food sources?

   _____

   _____

   _____

   _____

Communicating Results

Name: _____ Date: _____

Directions: Look at the chart. Graph how much energy is in a 100 g serving of different foods. Answer the question.

Food (100 g)	Energy (kcal)
lean beef	176
chicken breast	146
broccoli	34
strawberries	32
cheese	406
shrimp	99
brown rice	111

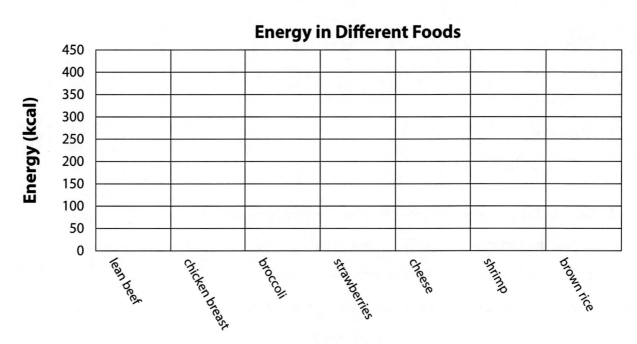

Energy in Different Foods

1. Which food has the most energy per 100 g? Which food has the least energy?

_____

_____

_____

Name: _____ **Date:** _____

Directions: Read the text, and answer the questions.

Down to Earth

Gravity is what keeps our feet firmly on the ground. On Earth, gravity pulls objects toward the center of the planet. This downward force is what makes something fall when you drop it. It's also what determines your weight. If you stand on a scale, gravity pulls you down against it. The scale shows your weight, which is the strength of this force.

Gravity works across space. This means that gravity is a force that works without objects having to touch each other. The sun's gravity pulls Earth, and Earth's gravity pulls the moon. This is why Earth continues to revolve around the sun, and the moon continues to revolve around Earth.

Learning Content

1. What is gravity?

   a. an upward force

   b. a lateral force

   c. a force that keeps our feet on the ground

   d. a force that pushes things away from each other

2. Which way does gravity pull objects on Earth?

   a. up away from Earth

   b. toward the center of Earth

   c. left

   d. right

3. Do objects have to touch each other for gravity to work?

   _____

   _____

4. Why do objects fall down after you throw them in the air?

   _____

   _____

Name: _____ Date: _____

Analyzing Data

Directions: Read the text, and study the chart. Then, answer the questions.

> Weight measures the force of gravity on an object. Your weight would be different on the moon because the gravity is not the same as on Earth.
>
> The chart shows how gravity on Earth compares to other locations. If Earth's gravity is 1, then a number higher than one means the force of gravity is stronger than on Earth. If the number is lower than 1, the force of gravity is weaker than on Earth.

Location	Gravity
Earth	1
outer space	0
Earth's moon	0.17
Venus	0.90
Mars	0.38
Mercury	0.38
Jupiter	2.36
Saturn	0.92
Uranus	0.89
Neptune	1.13

1. Which planet has the strongest gravity?

   a. Neptune   b. Jupiter

   c. Saturn   d. Venus

2. Where would you have no weight at all?

   a. outer space   b. Uranus

   c. Mercury   d. Mars

3. On which planet would you weigh the least?

   a. Earth   b. Mercury

   c. Neptune   d. Jupiter

Developing Questions

Name: _____ **Date:** _____

Directions: Read the text, and answer the questions.

December 1972 was the last time that people walked on the moon. The gravity on the moon is only 17 percent of the gravity on Earth. On Earth, you can probably jump 0.46 meters (1.5 feet), and the jump would last one second. If you jump with the same force on the moon, you could jump about 3 meters (10 feet) off the ground, and the jump would last four seconds.

1. Why are you able to jump higher on the moon?

_____

_____

_____

2. If you jumped on a planet with more gravity than Earth, could you jump higher?

    a. Yes, there wouldn't be as much downward force.

    b. No, there would be more downward force.

    c. Yes, there would be more downward force.

    d. No, there wouldn't be as much downward force.

3. What is a question you can ask about how gravity affects you?

_____

_____

_____

_____

Planning Solutions

Name: _____   Date: _____

Directions: Read the text, and answer the questions.

Cory is creating an experiment to see how gravity affects different objects. He has two balls that are the same size and shape. One ball is heavier than the other. Because the balls are the same shape, air resistance will affect them the same way. Air resistance is the force of air against an object. It slows objects down when they are falling. Cory stands on a ladder and drops the balls at the same time. They hit the ground at the same time.

1. What does it tell Cory when the balls hit the ground at the same time?

   a. Gravity causes the balls to fall at the same speed.

   b. Gravity causes the balls to fall at different speeds.

   c. Gravity does not affect the balls at all.

   d. Air resistance affects each ball differently.

2. Do you think he would get different results with objects that are different shapes?

   a. Yes, air resistance would affect them differently.

   b. No, air resistance would affect them the same way.

   c. Yes, but only if they are different colors.

   d. No, air resistance does not affect falling objects.

3. How can Cory create an experiment to test how different types of objects fall toward Earth?

   _____

   _____

   _____

   _____

Name: _____ **Date:** _____

Directions: Read the text. Fill out the chart, and answer the question.

> Mass is how much matter is in an object. Mass can be measured in kilograms (kg). Your weight can also be measured in kilograms. Use this formula to figure out what the weight of a 35 kg (75 lb.) child would be on other planets: mass × gravity = weight.

Location	Mass (kg)	Gravity	Weight (kg)
Earth	35	1	35
outer space	35	0	0
Earth's moon	35	0.17	
Venus	35	0.90	
Mars	35	0.38	
Mercury	35	0.38	
Jupiter	35	2.36	
Saturn	35	0.92	
Uranus	35	0.89	
Neptune	35	1.13	

1. On which planet would this child weigh the most?

_____

2. On which planet would it be the hardest to jump?

_____

3. Where would you float?

_____

4. Where would you be able to jump the highest? Why?

_____

_____

Communicating Results

Learning Content

Name: _____ Date: _____

Directions: Read the text, and answer the questions.

Oceans and Ecosystems

Earth has four major systems. The geosphere is soil, rocks, and molten rocks. The atmosphere is air. The biosphere is all living things. The hydrosphere is all the water and ice on Earth. Earth's oceans make up a large part of the hydrosphere, and they are home to many ecosystems and living things.

Different areas of the ocean have different types of ecosystems. The characteristics of each one are the result of the physical factors that create them. Temperature, tides, light availability, and where in the planet the oceans are located all affect them. Areas of the ocean that are near the shore are usually teeming with life. Others, like the very deep, dark regions of the ocean, have only small pockets of life that are spread far apart.

1. What is the hydrosphere?

    a. soil and rocks

    b. water and ice

    c. air

    d. living things

2. What are some physical factors that affect the ocean ecosystems?

    a. tides

    b. light availability

    c. temperature

    d. all of the above

3. Deep-sea ecosystems have _____ life spread far apart.

    a. pockets of

    b. lots of

    c. no

    d. many kinds of

51411—180 Days of Science

© *Shell Education*

Name: _____ **Date:** _____

Directions: Read the text. Look at the diagram and chart. Then, answer the questions.

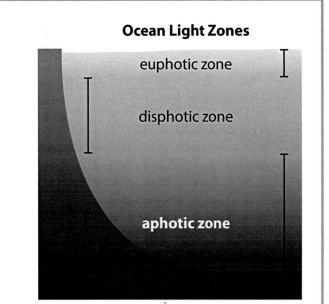

Ocean Light Zones

euphotic zone

disphotic zone

aphotic zone

There are three zones of the ocean. Each has a different ecosystem.

Analyzing Data

Zone	Description
euphotic	lots of sunlight, most of the living things
disphotic	some sunlight, but not enough for plants to survive
aphotic	no light at all, very cold, few animals

1. Where do most of the ocean plants and animals live?

   a. euphotic zone

   b. aphotic zone

   c. disphotic zone

   d. shore

2. Which zone would be most difficult for humans to explore?

   a. disphotic zone

   b. aphotic zone

   c. euphotic zone

   d. They are all easy to explore.

3. Where is there some sunlight but not enough for plants?

   a. aphotic zone

   b. disphotic zone

   c. euphotic zone

   d. There is sunlight in all of the ocean.

Name: _____ **Date:** _____

Directions: Read the text, and answer the questions.

Moses is visiting the aquarium with his family. He is looking at a display about ocean plants. He learns that 70 percent of Earth's oxygen is made by plants that live in the water. Plants release oxygen during photosynthesis, which is how plants make their food. Plants need light for photosynthesis. Even though they live in the water, they still get enough light to make oxygen.

Developing Questions

1. If ocean plants are hurt by pollution or rising water temperatures, what could happen?

    a. Less oxygen is put into the air.

    b. More oxygen is put into the air.

    c. The same amount of oxygen is put into the air.

    d. There would be no more oxygen.

2. Where in the ocean must marine plants live?

    a. at the top where there is a lot of light

    b. where there is limited light

    c. where there is no light

    d. any place

3. What happens during photosynthesis?

    a. Plants release oxygen.

    b. Plants use oxygen.

    c. Plants drink water.

    d. Plants eat food.

4. What is a question you can ask about the oxygen produced by ocean plants?

    _____

    _____

51411—180 Days of Science   © *Shell Education*

Planning Solutions

Name: _____ **Date:** _____

Directions: Read the text, and answer the questions.

Moses is visiting the aquarium with his family. He sees a display about deep-sea creatures.

The deepest part of the ocean is over 10,900 meters (36,000 feet) deep. This is deeper than Mount Everest is tall. We know less about the deep sea than any other habitat on Earth. The ocean is so deep that sunlight cannot reach where these deep-sea creatures live. This means it is very dark and cold. Some creatures, like the anglerfish, have special body parts that allow them to produce their own light to attract prey.

Moses wants to know more about how creatures survive in the deep sea.

1. Why don't we know more about the ocean?

   a. It is too deep.

   b. It is too dark.

   c. It is too cold.

   d. all of the above

2. How does the anglerfish attract prey?

   a. with its eyes

   b. with its teeth

   c. with the light it makes

   d. with its fins

3. How can Moses create a model of the ocean and the different ecosystems?

_____

_____

_____

_____

Name: _____ **Date:** _____

Directions: Read the text. Sort items from the word bank into the correct zones. Answer the questions.

no sunlight	dim light	coldest water
bright sunlight	very few animals	warmest water
lots of animals	colder water	few animals

Ocean Light Zones

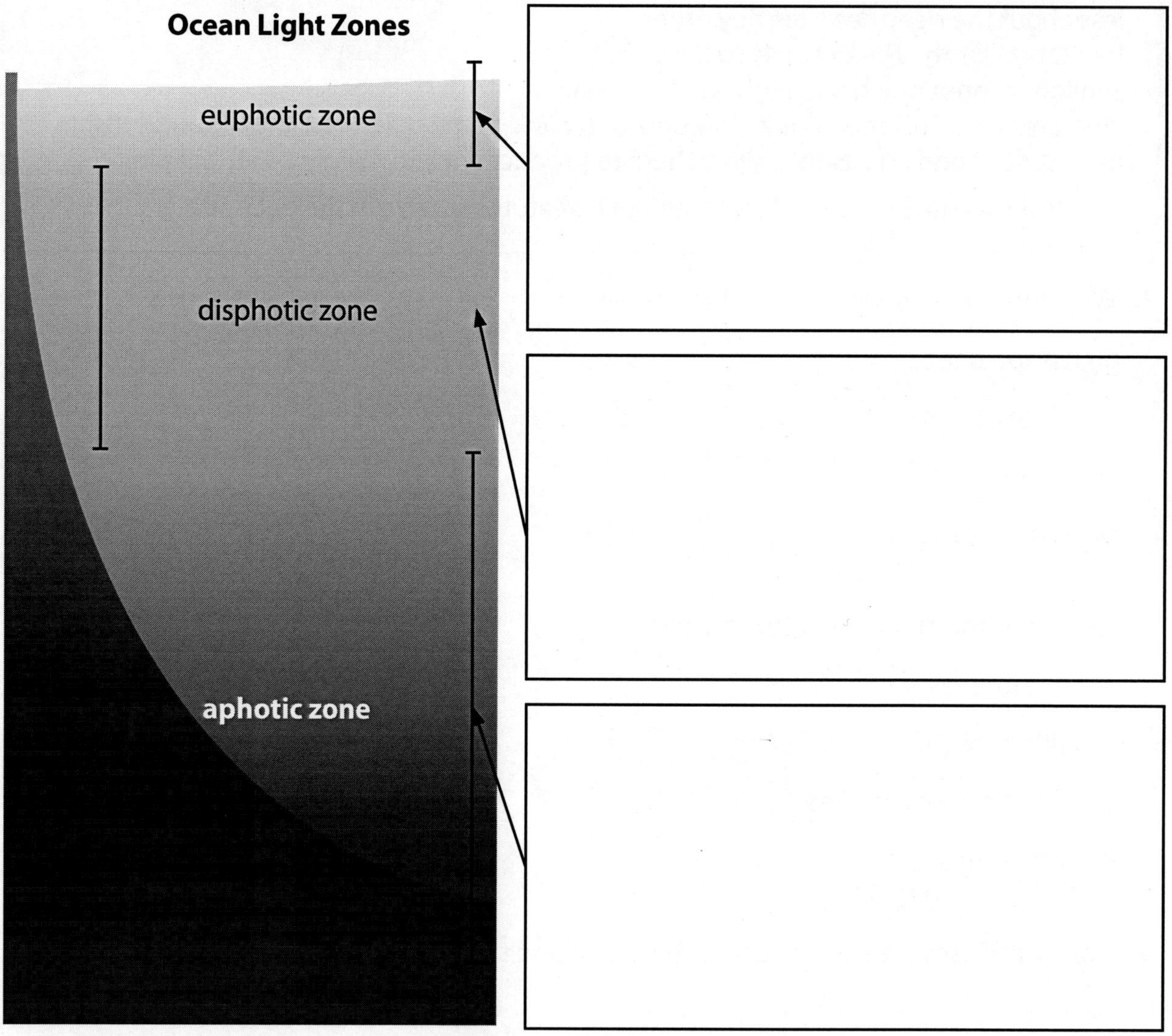

euphotic zone

disphotic zone

aphotic zone

1. What is unique about the aphotic zone?

_____

_____

_____

Name: _____ **Date:** _____

Directions: Read the text, and answer the questions.

Winds and Clouds in Mountain Ranges

The atmosphere is air, which is the combination of gases that surround Earth. Believe it or not, mountains have a huge impact on the way that our atmosphere behaves. They affect the formation of clouds and the way that wind blows. This means that they affect the overall climate of an area. When wind blows across a mountain range, air rises and cools. This causes moisture in the air to condense and clouds to form. This influences the amount of rain or snow in a mountain climate.

Usually, the side of the mountain where the wind blows is the wetter side of the mountain. The other side of the mountain is called the "rain shadow." It is much drier because the mountains block the rain-producing clouds.

Learning Content

1. What is the atmosphere?

   a. mountains   **b.** air

   c. sunlight   **d.** trees

2. What happens to wind when it blows across a mountain range?

   a. It rises and cools.   **b.** It rises and warms.

   c. It falls and cools.   **d.** Nothing changes.

3. How do mountains affect the formation of clouds?

   _____

   _____

   _____

   _____

Analyzing Data

Name: _____ **Date:** _____

Directions: Read the text, and look at the diagram. Answer the questions.

> The windward side of the mountain faces the wind. The leeward side is the side of the mountain that is downwind. There is less wind on this side because it is blocked by the mountain on the other side. The leeward side of a mountain is usually dry compared to the windward side.

windward side   air rises, cools, and condenses   leeward side

wind

1. Why do clouds form on the windward side of a mountain?

   a. The air rises, cools, and condenses.   **b.** Clouds blow from somewhere else.

   c. The air rises and warms.   **d.** They form on the leeward side.

2. What is different about the leeward side of the mountain?

   a. It is wetter.   **b.** It is drier.

   c. It is steeper.   **d.** It is more slippery.

3. Is the climate different on the windward side? How do you know?

   _____

   _____

   _____

4. Do you think there would be different animals that live on the leeward side? Why or why not?

   _____

   _____

   _____

Developing Questions

Name: _____ **Date:** _____

Directions: Read the text, and answer the questions.

Jeff is studying mountain climates. He discovers that the bottom of mountains are usually lush forests on the wetter side of the mountain. As you travel up the mountain, it gets much colder. Above the "tree line," the plants are much smaller. The top of a mountain is usually just snow-covered rocks. The air at the top of a mountain is too thin for people to breathe easily.

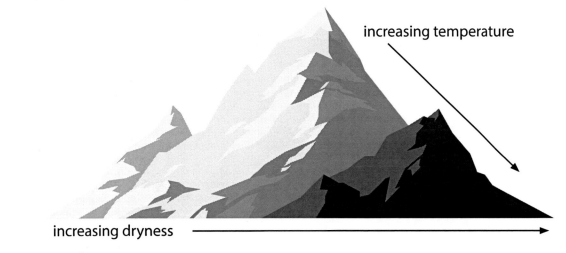

increasing temperature

increasing dryness

1. Why does one side of the bottom of mountains have more plants?

   a. There is a lot of rain.   **b.** It is very dry.

   c. It is very cold.   **d.** The air is thin.

2. Why aren't there plants at the top of a tall mountain?

   a. It is too cold.   **b.** It is too wet.

   c. There are too many animals.   **d.** The air is too thick.

3. What could Jeff ask about the different mountain climates?

   _____

   _____

   _____

   _____

Planning Solutions

Name: _____ **Date:** _____

Directions: Read the text, and answer the questions.

> Shelia is studying mountains and learns about the rain shadow. The area in the rain shadow gets much less rain than the other side. This is caused when wind blows up the windward side of the mountain and forms clouds. The clouds cause precipitation on the windward side and leave the leeward side much drier. She wants to make a model of the rain shadow.

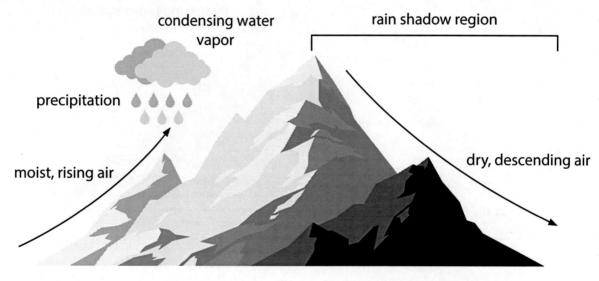

1. What is the rain shadow?

   a. the wet windward side

   b. the dry leeward side

   c. the cold windward side

   d. the lush leeward side

2. What might the climate in the rain shadow be like?

   a. desert

   b. rainforest

   c. pine forest

   d. ocean

3. Describe how Shelia can build a model of a mountain and its rain shadow using paper, paint, and clay.

   _____

   _____

   _____

   _____

Name: ______________________ Date: ______________

Directions: Draw a mountain, wind, clouds, and rain. Show how the wind and clouds affect the climate. Label your picture, and answer the question.

Communicating Results

1. Explain what is happening in your picture.

____

____

____

Learning Content

Name: _____ **Date:** _____

Directions: Read the text, and answer the questions.

Rivers and Lakes

Seventy percent of Earth's surface is covered in water. This might seem like more than enough for all our needs. The truth is, 97 percent of the available water on Earth is salt water in oceans. We use mainly fresh water, which is far less available. Most of Earth's fresh water is underground or frozen in glaciers. This means that only a fraction of fresh water is available to us in rivers and lakes. Because of this, we have to use our water carefully. It is a finite resource, and humans must take care not to pollute or waste the water we have.

1. Where is most of Earth's fresh water?

   a. underground or frozen   **b.** in oceans or frozen

   c. in rivers and lakes   **d.** in the atmosphere

2. What kind of water is 97 percent of water on Earth?

   a. fresh water   **b.** salt water

   c. frozen water   **d.** water vapor

3. Where does most of the water we use come from?

   _____

   _____

4. Why should humans not waste water?

   _____

   _____

51411—180 Days of Science

Name: _____ **Date:** _____

Directions: Read the text, and look at the charts. Then, answer the questions.

Only three percent of Earth's water is fresh water. Most of it is not available to us. Most of the water we use comes from rivers and lakes.

All Water on Earth

Fresh Water 3%

Salt Water 97%

Fresh Water

Lakes, Rivers, and Swamps 0.9%

Groundwater 30.1%

Icecaps and Glaciers 68.7%

1. What is most of Earth's water?

   a. fresh water   **b.** groundwater

   c. salt water   **d.** lakes

2. Most of Earth's fresh water is _____ .

   a. frozen   **b.** salty

   c. swamps   **d.** groundwater

3. Where does most of the water we use come from?

   a. oceans and glaciers **b.** glaciers and rivers

   c. swamps and lakes   **d.** rivers and lakes

4. What percentage of fresh water is in lakes, rivers, and swamps?

   _____

5. Do you think we can use groundwater? Why or why not?

   _____

   _____

Name: _____ **Date:** _____

Directions: Read the text, and answer the questions.

Developing Questions

    Felix is creating a model to show how much of Earth's water exists in different places. He has a total of 1,000 mL of water. This represents all the water on Earth. He puts 970 mL of water in a bottle to represent all the salt water.

1. How much water does Felix have left to represent all the fresh water on Earth?

    a. 30 mL

    b. 3 mL

    c. 300 mL

    d. 3,000 mL

2. Only a very tiny amount of Earth's water is in the atmosphere as water vapor. How much water should be put in a cup to represent this?

    a. a drop

    b. 10 mL

    c. 20 mL

    d. 30 mL

3. What can you ask about creating a model to represent the breakdown of fresh water?

_____

_____

_____

Name: _____ Date: _____

Directions: Read the text, and answer the questions.

Greta is creating a model to represent all of the fresh water in the world. She has 1,000 mL of water. She freezes 687 mL to represent the ice caps and glaciers. She puts 301 mL in a jar with a lid to represent groundwater. She puts 3 mL in a cup to represent surface water. The rest of the water is soil moisture and water vapor in the atmosphere.

1. How much water should she put in a cup to represent soil moisture and water vapor?

   a. 0.9 mL   **b.** 9 mL

   c. 90 mL   **d.** 900 mL

2. This model helps show Greta that we have _____ fresh water that we can use.

   a. very little   **b.** a lot

   c. unlimited   **d.** 3 mL

3. How can Greta represent the distribution of water in another way?

   _____

   _____

   _____

   _____

Communicating Results

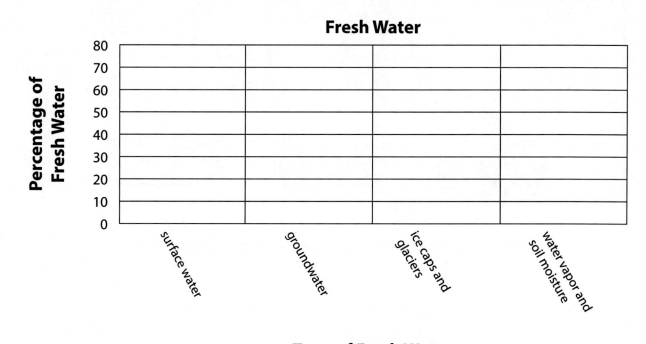

Name: _____ **Date:** _____

Directions: Graph the data in the chart. Then, answer the questions.

Type of Fresh Water	Percentage of Total Fresh Water
surface water (lakes, rivers, swamps)	0.3
groundwater	30.1
ice caps and glaciers	68.7
water vapor and soil moisture	0.9

Fresh Water

Percentage of Fresh Water

80
70
60
50
40
30
20
10
0

surface water   groundwater   ice caps and glaciers   water vapor and soil moisture

Type of Fresh Water

1. Why do you think it is important to conserve water?

_____

_____

2. Where is the majority of Earth's fresh water? Why is this important?

_____

_____

_____

Name: _____ **Date:** _____

Directions: Read the text, and answer the questions.

The Polar Ice Caps

The polar ice caps cover Earth's north and south poles. They have existed for millions of years and stay frozen all year. The temperatures are much lower than in other places. Both the North Pole and the South Pole experience six months each year where the sun does not rise above the horizon. This means it is either twilight or dark during this time. When the sun is above the horizon, most of the sunlight is reflected by the bright white surface.

The average winter temperature at the North Pole is –40° C (–40° F). The average winter temperature at the South Pole is –60° C (–76° F). The South Pole gets colder because the ice is on the continent Antarctica. The continent and the ice sheet are at a very high elevation. The ice cap in the North Pole sits in the middle of the Arctic Ocean. It also covers parts of several countries, including Greenland. The ice caps make up nearly 70 percent of Earth's fresh water, and 90 percent of this is in Antarctica.

1. Why is the South Pole colder than the North Pole?

    a. It is at a higher elevation.   **b.** It is at a lower elevation.

    c. It is darker there.   **d.** It is not colder.

2. Most of the sunlight that the ice caps get is _____ .

    a. absorbed by the bright white surface   **b.** reflected by the bright white surface

    c. absorbed by the six months of darkness and twilight   **d.** blocked by the high elevation

3. Do you think we can use the fresh water in the ice caps? Why or why not?

    _____

    _____

    _____

Learning Content

Analyzing Data

Name: _____ Date: _____

Directions: Read the text, and look at the chart. Then, answer the questions.

The Arctic and the Antarctic are often thought of as the same. They are both cold, dark, and remote. They do have many differences, though. The thickness of the ice and area covered can change depending on the temperature. The ice never completely melts, though. The chart shows the largest area that can be covered by the ice and how thick it is on average.

Polar Ice Cap	Average Maximum Area Covered (km²)	Average Ice Thickness (m)	Average Winter Temperature
northern (Arctic)	15.6 million	2	−40° C
southern (Antarctic)	18.8 million	1	−60° C

1. Why does the area covered by ice change?

   a. The temperature stays the same.   b. The temperature changes.

   c. People chip away at the ice.   d. Animals break the ice.

2. How many square kilometers of ice can be in the Antarctic?

   a. 18.8 million   b. 15.6 million

   c. 90 million   d. 12 million

3. Where is the ice thicker?

   a. Arctic   b. Antarctic

   c. They are the same.   d. There is no way to measure it.

4. Do you think the average winter temperature affects the area covered by ice? Why or why not?

   _____

   _____

   _____

51411—180 Days of Science

Name: _____ Date: _____

Directions: Read the text, and answer the questions.

> Aria is learning about the polar ice caps. She learns that they can affect the climate a lot if they melt. She decides to make a model of how melting ice can affect sea levels. She has water, paper cups, sand, and a large, shallow tray.

1. How can Aria represent a polar ice cap?

   a. Freeze a cup of water.

   b. Put sand into the cup.

   c. Fill the tray with sand.

   d. Fill the tray with water.

2. How can Aria represent the land and ocean?

   a. Fill the tray with sand, and build a mountain with it.

   b. Fill the tray with water until it overflows.

   c. Build sand up in half the tray, and fill the rest with water.

   d. Freeze a tray of water.

3. What is a question Aria can ask about the model she is making?

   _____

   _____

   _____

4. What can Aria learn from her model?

   _____

   _____

   _____

Developing Questions

Name: _____ **Date:** _____

Directions: Read the text, and answer the questions.

> Aria is learning about the polar ice caps. She is building a model. She fills a shallow tray halfway with sand and adds water to represent the ocean. She freezes a paper cup of water, removes the ice from the cup, and sets it in the tray to represent an ice cap. She is going to monitor the water levels as the ice melts.

Planning Solutions

1. What will happen as the ice melts?

   a. The ice won't melt.

   b. The water will stay the same.

   c. The water will recede.

   d. The water will rise.

2. How could melting polar ice caps affect the animals that live on them?

   a. reduces their habitat

   b. affects food sources

   c. gives animals more room to play

   d. both a and b

3. How can Aria improve her model to show how the melting ice can affect animals and shorelines?

   _____

   _____

   _____

   _____

Name: _____ **Date:** _____

Directions: Temperatures in the Arctic have been rising bit by bit. Look at the graph, and answer the questions.

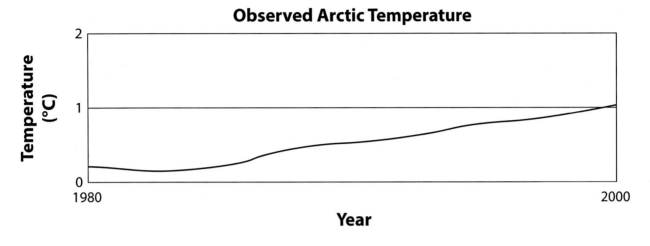

Communicating Results

1. Why might rising temperatures affect animals in the Arctic?

_____

_____

_____

_____

2. How might rising temperatures in the Arctic affect other parts of the world?

_____

_____

_____

_____

3. Do you think it is possible that temperatures will start to go back down? Why or why not?

_____

_____

_____

_____

Learning Content

Name: _____ Date: _____

Directions: Read the text, and answer the questions.

Agriculture and Industry Improvements

Humans are always making changes to the world. We create farms to produce food. We build cities and factories. All these changes benefit people in many ways, but they can affect the world dramatically. Our changes can harm the world. They can destroy animal habitats and harm our soil. They can pollute the air and water. People realize now that we must take care of our resources and do things to protect our environment. Many improvements have been made to farming and industry over the years. Many farmers now take steps to improve farming practices, such as rotating crops and preventing erosion. Laws are also in place to help protect the air and water from pollution.

1. Farming and industry can _____ the environment.

   a. light up   **b.** harm

   c. burn   **d.** freeze

2. People have taken steps to make sure that farming and industry practices
   _____ .

   a. harm the environment less   **b.** harm the environment more

   c. are worse than ever   **d.** haven't changed

3. What are some reasons we have environmental laws?

   a. They allow pollution of air and water.   **b.** They tell us where to put our chemicals.

   c. They tell us the right kind of pollution to make.   **d.** They reduce pollution of air and water.

4. What are some things that have improved in farming practices?

   _____

   _____

Analyzing Data

Name: _____ **Date:** _____

Directions: Read the text, and look at the chart. Then, answer the questions.

Industrial farming has been the standard for decades. This means large farms grow the same crops every year. They often use harmful pesticides and fertilizers. Now there are many farmers that try to take care of the natural resources we have. Sustainable agriculture uses practices that protect the environment, animals, and people.

Sustainable Agriculture Practice	Definition
rotating crops	planting a variety of crops to keep soil healthy and improve pest control
planting cover crops	planting crops during off season to protect the soil and prevent erosion
reducing or eliminating tillage	reducing or eliminating plowing to reduce soil loss
applying integrated pest management	keeps pests under control while minimizing use of chemical pesticides
agroforestry practices	mixing trees and shrubs into farms to shelter and protect plants, animals, and water resources

1. What is the benefit of crop rotation?

   a. reduced erosion   b. healthy soil

   c. protected animals   d. protected water

2. Agroforestry practices means mixing _____ into farms.

   a. grass   b. animals

   c. trees   d. ladybugs

3. What is the benefit of reducing tillage?

   a. less soil loss   b. more soil loss

   c. fewer bugs   d. fewer cows

4. Which practice minimizes the use of chemical pesticides?

   _____

   _____

Developing Questions

Name: _____ Date: _____

Directions: Read the text, and answer the questions.

Jacob lives on a farm. The farm has livestock. The animals don't have any shelter from the sun or rain. Jacob's family decides to plant some fruit trees on the land as well.

1. How do the trees benefit the livestock?

    a. They provide shelter.

    b. They provide wood.

    c. They provide fertilizer.

    d. They provide grass.

2. How do the trees benefit the farm owners?

    a. They will have no shade.

    b. They can sell the fruit.

    c. The trees will block their view.

    d. The trees will keep their cows from eating.

3. What is a question you could ask about the benefits of having trees and livestock on one farm?

    _____

    _____

    _____

    _____

Name: _____ Date: _____

Directions: Read the text, and answer the questions.

> Miya is studying laws that help protect the environment. She learns about the Clean Air Act of 1970. This law helps protect Earth from air pollution. It limits the amount of emissions, or harmful gasses, put into the air from factories and cars.

Planning Solutions

1. The Clean Air Act makes factories control their _____ .

    a. air pollution

    b. water pollution

    c. fertilizer use

    d. soil erosion

2. The Clean Air Act made car companies improve car _____ .

    a. paint

    b. emissions

    c. climate control

    d. top speeds

3. What are some ways that Miya can contribute to clean air in her own life?

_____

_____

_____

4. Some states require cars to be inspected before they are allowed on the road. What is one reason states might require this?

_____

_____

Communicating Results

Name: _____ Date: _____

Directions: The box lists farming and industry practices and some of the effects of different practices. Sort the items into the chart. Then, answer the questions.

crop rotation	reducing tillage	wasting water
chemical pesticide use	Clean Air Act of 1970	climate change
planting cover crops	soil erosion	habitat loss

Helpful	Harmful

1. How does the Clean Air Act of 1970 help our planet?

_____

_____

_____

2. Explain the effect of habitat loss on animals.

_____

_____

_____

Name: _____   **Date:** _____

Directions: Read the text, and answer the questions.

Protecting Our Water Sources

Only a small part of Earth's water is usable fresh water. It is a limited resource. This means that people must do what they can to protect the water we have. Many things can pollute our water sources. Water pollution occurs when harmful substances enter our groundwater, lakes, rivers, streams, or oceans.

There are many types of water pollution. You may have heard of oil spills happening in the ocean. These are large events that are very harmful to living things and the environment. There are many other types of water pollution that are less obvious. These can include sewage, fertilizer runoff, or even heat released into the water. Luckily, people have realized the harmful effects of different types of pollution. There are now laws in place to help protect our water.

Learning Content

1. What is pollution?

   a. slick substances

   b. cold substances

   c. helpful substances

   d. harmful substances

2. What are in place to help protect our water?

   a. laws

   b. gates

   c. pollutants

   d. humans

3. Which types of water can be polluted?

   a. groundwater

   b. oceans

   c. lakes

   d. all of the above

4. What are some different types of water pollution?

   _____

   _____

Name: _____ Date: _____

Analyzing Data

Directions: There are many ways that our water sources can become polluted. Look at the chart, and answer the questions.

Type of Water Pollution	Definition
oil spills	release of oil into the environment, especially the ocean
farm animal waste	waste from large herds of farm animals that can get into the water through storm runoff
pesticides and herbicides	harmful chemicals that can get into the water through storm runoff or accidental spills
thermal pollution	changing the temperature of the water, harmful to organisms in the water, often caused by factories
acid rain	rain that has harmful properties, caused by air pollution

1. Which type of water pollution is caused by air pollution?

    a. farm animal waste

    b. acid rain

    c. oil spills

    d. pesticides

2. Which type of pollution is the result of farming practices?

    a. farm animal waste and oil spills

    b. pesticides and oil spills

    c. acid rain

    d. farm animal waste and pesticides

3. What is thermal pollution?

    a. changing the temperature of water

    b. changing the location of a factory

    c. adding oil to the water

    d. adding pesticides to water

4. Which type of water pollution do you think is most harmful to animals? Why?

    _____

    _____

    _____

    _____

Name: _____ **Date:** _____

Directions: Read the text, and answer the questions.

Livia is taking a walk in the neighborhood with her dad. They live near a pond full of ducks and turtles. She sees one of the neighbors washing his car in the driveway. Soapy water is running down the street toward the pond.

1. If the soapy water reaches the pond, what will happen?

   a. It will clean the water.

   b. It will pollute the water.

   c. It will make the water better.

   d. Nothing will happen.

2. What could the neighbor do to help prevent the soapy water from entering the pond?

   a. Wash on an area that absorbs water, like grass or gravel.

   b. Use an environmentally-safe cleaner.

   c. Go to a commercial carwash.

   d. any of the above

3. What is a question you could ask about ways to protect our water?

   _____

   _____

4. If the pond becomes polluted, what could be some effects?

   _____

   _____

Planning Solutions

Name: _____ Date: _____

Directions: Read the text, and answer the questions.

> Lea is trying to find ways that she can protect water sources while she is at home. She notices that her parents are spraying weed killer in the backyard. She also sees her mom flushing old medicines down the toilet. She learned that these things can pollute the water.

1. Why might the weed killer be a problem?

   a. The chemicals will make the weeds grow taller.

   b. The chemicals will kill the grass.

   c. The chemicals can wash into a nearby pond.

   d. It is not a problem.

2. What can Lea do to help her parents so that they don't need weed killer.

   a. Pull the weeds.

   b. Water the weeds.

   c. Feed the weeds.

   d. Poison the weeds.

3. Why do you think flushing the medicine down the toilet could be a problem?

   _____

   _____

4. Make a plan for Lea to protect water at their home.

   _____

   _____

   _____

Name: _____ **Date:** _____

Directions: Create a sign that would tell people to stop polluting a certain water source, such as a lake or an ocean. Answer the question.

[blank box for drawing]

1. What does your sign mean?

_____

_____

_____

Learning Content

Name: _____ **Date:** _____

Directions: Read the text, and answer the questions.

Earth's Orbit

If you look at the sky often, you may notice that the sun, moon, and stars appear to change. They look like they move. However, most of these changes are the result of Earth moving. Earth and all the other planets in our solar system revolve around the sun. Although we are moving extremely fast through outer space, it still takes 365.24 days to revolve around the sun. Our trip around the sun, combined with Earth's tilt, causes our seasons. Day and night are caused by Earth spinning on its axis, which is an invisible line through the north and south poles. The moon also travels with us through space as it revolves around Earth.

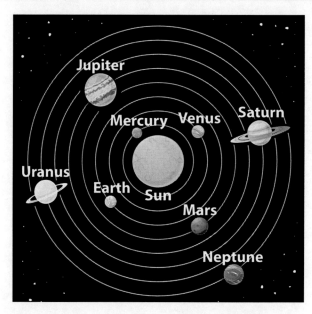

1. Earth and other planets _____ around the sun.

   a. rotate   **b.** revolve

   c. jump   **d.** float

2. What causes day and night?

   a. earth spinning on its axis   **b.** earth's orbit around the sun

   c. the sun revolving around earth   **d.** the moon blocking the sun

3. What revolves around Earth?

   a. Jupiter   **b.** the sun

   c. the moon   **d.** Saturn

Analyzing Data

Name: _____ **Date:** _____

Directions: Read the text and look at the diagram. Then, answer the questions.

> You may think that it is Earth's orbit that causes the seasons. It is really Earth's axial tilt. The axis is the invisible line that runs through the north and south poles. It is tilted about 23.5 degrees. It is actually winter in the Northern Hemisphere when Earth is closest to the sun.

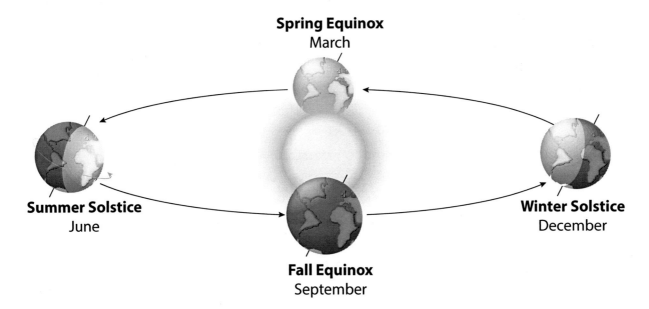

Spring Equinox
March

Summer Solstice
June

Winter Solstice
December

Fall Equinox
September

1. What month is it when Earth has the winter solstice?

a. March

b. June

c. January

d. December

2. What month is it when Earth has the spring equinox?

a. July

b. September

c. March

d. June

3. Explain how Earth's tilt affects the seasons.

_____

_____

_____

Name: _____   **Date:** _____

Developing Questions

Directions: Read the text, and answer the questions.

Weston's classroom is doing an activity to demonstrate how Earth revolves around the sun. They have pie pans, balls of clay, and a ball. They stick the clay to the middle of the pie pan, and they put the ball in the pan as well.

1. When you tilt the pan in a circular motion, what will happen?

   a. The ball will roll into the clay.   **b.** The ball will roll around the edge.

   c. The clay will roll around the ball.   **d.** Nothing will happen.

2. If you want the model to be in proportion, how should the size of the ball compare to the size of the clay?

   a. much smaller   **b.** much larger

   c. same size   **d.** a little larger

3. What is a question you could ask about the relationship between Earth and the sun?

   _____

   _____

   _____

4. What is another way that you could model Earth revolving around the sun?

   _____

   _____

   _____

   _____

Name: _____ **Date:** _____

Directions: Read the text, and answer the questions.

Weston and his class go out to the playground to draw a model of Earth's orbit around the sun. They use yellow chalk to draw a big circle that represents the sun. Then they measure one meter from the sun and draw a smaller blue circle to represent Earth. They tie a one-meter piece of string to the chalk. One person holds the end of string down in the middle of the "sun", and another person drags the chalk in a circle around the sun. This represents Earth's orbit.

1. What should they add to the diagram to make it more accurate?

    a. Earth's moon

    b. the sun's moon

    c. a bigger circle for Earth

    d. They should make the sun green.

2. How could Weston make this into an accurate model of the whole solar system?

    a. Draw additional planets and circles to represent their orbits.

    b. Draw planets without circles for orbits.

    c. Draw more stars.

    d. Draw comets.

3. Describe how Weston should walk around the chalk sun to represent the way that Earth spins as it rotates. What could he do to represent the moon?

    _____

    _____

    _____

    _____

    _____

Planning Solutions

Name: _____ **Date:** _____

Directions: Draw Earth's orbit around the sun. Include Earth's tilt and its moon. Label your picture.

Communicating Results

1. What are the effects of Earth's tilt?

_____

_____

Name: _____ **Date:** _____

Directions: Read the text, and answer the questions.

Day and Night on Earth

Earth spins on its axis, which is an invisible line that connects the north and south poles. The axis isn't straight up and down, though. It is tilted at about 23.5 degrees. Earth takes 24 hours to complete one rotation on its axis. It is this spinning that causes us to experience day and night. Although it looks like the sun rises and sets, it's our spinning that makes it look this way. When it is day where you live, your part of the world is facing the sun. When it is night, your part of the world is facing away from the sun. It is always daytime somewhere on the planet.

Time zones are also related to Earth's rotation. They standardize time for everyone on the planet. If we did not have time zones, noon would be in the middle of the day for some people and the middle of the night for others!

Learning Content

1. Earth spins on its _____ .

   a. revolution

   b. rotation

   c. axis

   d. line

2. How tilted is Earth?

   a. 23.5 degrees

   b. 45 degrees

   c. 30 degrees

   d. 180 degrees

3. What do we see because of Earth's rotation?

   a. clouds

   b. seasons

   c. sunrise and sunset

   d. constellations

4. Why do we have time zones?

_____

_____

Analyzing Data

Name: _____ **Date:** _____

Directions: Read the text, and look at the diagram. Then, answer the questions.

> The moon, sun, stars, and Earth are all related. Earth revolves around the sun, and the moon revolves around Earth. Meanwhile, Earth is also spinning on its axis. The spinning causes the sun, moon, and stars to look like they rise and set.

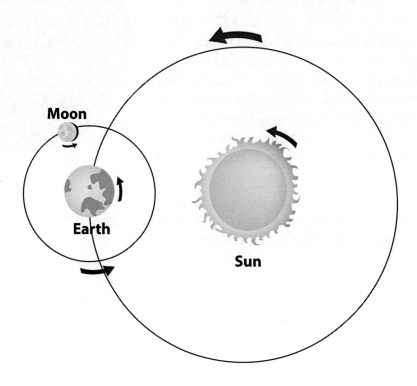

1. On what part of Earth is it daytime?

   a. the part facing the sun

   b. the part facing away from the sun

   c. the part where you can see the stars

   d. the part where it is dark

2. What part of the world can see the moon?

   a. the part facing the moon

   b. the part facing away from the moon

   c. the part where there is no moon

   d. the part that can't look outside

3. What do you think makes it look like the stars move across the sky?

   _____

   _____

   _____

Name: _____ **Date:** _____

Directions: Read the text, and answer the questions.

Kendra and Chelsea want to show how Earth's rotation creates day and night. Kendra stands holding a large ball to represent the sun. Chelsea stands a few meters away holding a globe to represent Earth.

1. What should Chelsea do to show how night and day happen?

   a. Walk around Kendra in a circle.　　**b.** Spin the globe.

   c. Toss the globe to Kendra.　　**d.** Walk closer to Kendra.

2. Ben is going to join in and represent the moon. What should he do?

   a. Walk around Chelsea.　　**b.** Walk around Kendra.

   c. Walk toward Kendra.　　**d.** Walk away from Chelsea.

3. What is a question you could ask about the moon revolving around Earth?

   _____

   _____

   _____

4. If Kendra held a lamp instead of a ball, what would this help them see?

   _____

   _____

   _____

Developing Questions

Name: _____   **Date:** _____

Directions: Read the text, and answer the questions.

We have time zones because the world spins on its axis. Time zones ensure that no matter where you live, your noon is the middle of the day when the sun is at its highest. Riku lives in New York and has family in Tokyo, Japan. Tokyo's time zone is 14 hours ahead of New York's.

1. What time should Riku call his family so that it is convenient for everyone?

   a. 7:00 a.m.

   b. noon

   c. 2:00 p.m.

   d. 10:00 a.m.

2. Is there ever a time that they could talk when the sun is up for both of them?

   a. Yes, during the summer when days are long.

   b. Yes, during the winter when days are short.

   c. Yes, during leap year only.

   d. No, this is never possible.

3. Make a plan for Riku to talk to his family when it is a different calendar day in Tokyo than it is in New York.

   _____

   _____

   _____

4. Do you think it would be difficult to travel between time zones? Why or why not?

   _____

   _____

Name: _____ **Date:** _____

Directions: Draw the sun, Earth, and the moon. Use arrows to show orbits and rotations. Answer the question.

1. Explain why we have day and night.

_____

_____

_____

Learning Content

Name: _____ **Date:** _____

Directions: Read the text, and answer the questions.

The Sun: Our Brightest Star?

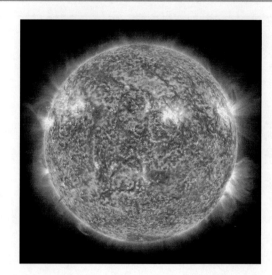

You have probably looked up at the stars more than once. They cover the sky in unequal groupings. Some stars seem bright, and some seem faint. Maybe you've even tried to find the brightest star in the sky. It turns out that our sun is actually the brightest star to us. How bright a star looks to us from Earth is different from how bright the star actually is.

Our sun is so massive that it warms our planet from 149.6 million kilometers (92.96 million miles) away. There are actually stars far larger and brighter than our sun, but they are so far away that they look like tiny points of light in the night sky. Imagine if you had one bright lamp and one dim lamp. If you put the dimmer lamp next to you and the brighter lamp down the street, the dimmer lamp will still look brighter from where you are.

1. How far away is the sun?

    a. 150 million kilometers   **b.** 14 million kilometers

    c. 149.6 million kilometers   **d.** 4 million kilometers

2. What is the sun?

    a. a planet   **b.** a comet

    c. a star   **d.** an asteroid

3. Is our sun the biggest star in the universe? How do you know?

_____

_____

4. Are how bright a star looks to us and how bright a star actually is the same thing? Explain.

_____

_____

Name: _____ **Date:** _____

Directions: Read the text, and look at the chart. Then, answer the questions.

> There are two ways to talk about how bright a star is. One is is how bright a star looks from Earth. The other is how bright the star actually is. Because the sun is our closest star, it will always look the brightest from Earth. There are much brighter stars but they are farther away.

Analyzing Data

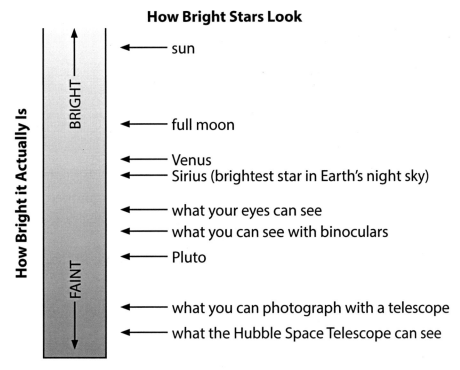

How Bright Stars Look

- sun
- full moon
- Venus
- Sirius (brightest star in Earth's night sky)
- what your eyes can see
- what you can see with binoculars
- Pluto
- what you can photograph with a telescope
- what the Hubble Space Telescope can see

How Bright it Actually Is BRIGHT — FAINT

1. After the sun, what is the brightest star we can see?

   a. full moon   b. Venus

   c. Sirius   d. Pluto

2. Would we ever be able to see Pluto without a telescope? Why or why not?

   _____

   _____

3. Do you think there are stars we cannot see with the Hubble Space Telescope? Why or why not?

   _____

   _____

Name: _____ **Date:** _____

Developing Questions

Directions: Read the text, and answer the questions.

Emilio looks outside at night. He sees the moon, which is very bright. He also sees many stars. Some of them are very bright, and some are so faint that he can hardly see them. He knows that Sirius is the brightest star in Earth's night sky. He can find Sirius by using the belt of the constellation Orion.

1. Can Emilio tell which stars are actually the brightest by looking at them from Earth?

   a. Yes, we can see how bright stars actually are from Earth.

   b. No, how bright stars are from Earth is different than how bright they actually are.

   c. Yes, how bright they actually are and the way they look from Earth are the same.

   d. No, he needs a telescope for that.

2. If Emilio wants to find Sirius, what would make it easier?

   a. knowing what the constellation Orion looks like

   b. knowing how to find the North Star

   c. knowing how to find the Big Dipper

   d. knowing what the Big Dipper looks like

3. What can Emilio ask about the easiest way to find Sirius?

   _____

   _____

   _____

   _____

Name: _____ **Date:** _____

Directions: Read the text, and answer the questions.

Emilio loves looking at the stars. He knows the brightest star we can see in the night sky is called Sirius. He heard that you can find Sirius because Orion's belt points to it. He looked up the constellation Orion and knows what it looks like.

1. Based on the image, when Emilio finds Orion, which way should he look to find Sirius?

    a. up from Orion's belt

    b. down from Orion's belt

    c. to the left of Orion's belt

    d. to the right of Orion's belt

2. What is the benefit of being able to recognize constellations in the sky?

    a. They tell you what time the moon set.

    b. They tell you what time the sun will rise.

    c. They help you find other objects in the sky.

    d. There is no benefit.

3. Emilio knows there is another bright star called the North Star that is attached to a constellation. Make a plan for Emilio to find the North Star.

    _____

    _____

    _____

Planning Solutions

Name: _____ **Date:** _____

Directions: Look at the picture. Tally the stars you see on the tally chart. Add a scale to the graph, and graph the stars you tallied.

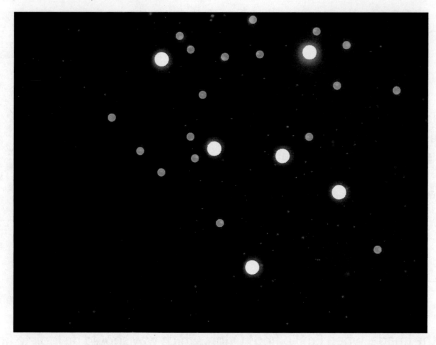

Tally Chart	
Brightness of Stars	**Number of Stars**
faint	
bright	

Number of Faint and Bright Stars

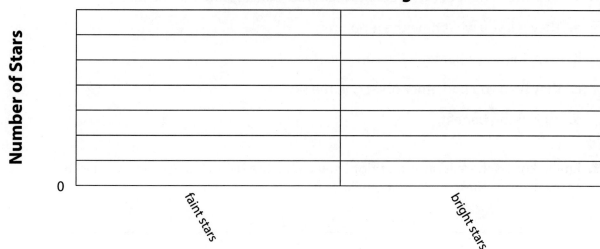

Number of Stars

0

faint stars   bright stars

Brightness of Stars

51411—180 Days of Science

Name: _____ **Date:** _____

Directions: Read the text, and answer the questions.

Chasing the Stars

Earth spinning on its axis causes the sun and moon to look like they rise and set. It also makes the stars look like they move slowly across the sky at night. Because the stars are so far away, this movement is not as dramatic as it is with the sun or moon. We can still see changes if we watch for them, though. The stars rise in the east and set in the west, just like the sun. There are ways to observe the motion of the stars over time. You can track the time that certain constellations rise each night. You can use landmarks to see how far certain stars move after a few hours. You can even take a special type of photograph that will show you the motion of the stars.

Learning Content

1. The stars _____ and _____ like the sun and moon.

    a. rise, set

    b. rise, rotate

    c. rise, revolve

    d. east, west

2. The stars rise in the _____ .

    a. south

    b. north

    c. east

    d. west

3. Can you observe the motion of the stars?

    a. Yes, they move quickly.

    c. Yes, there are several ways.

    b. No, they move too slowly.

    d. Yes, there is only one way.

Analyzing Data

Name: _____ **Date:** _____

Directions: Read the text, and look at the chart. Then, answer the questions.

> The sun rises and sets at a different time each day. Likewise, the stars rise and set at different times each day. The chart below shows the rise and set of Sirius over a ten-day period in Houston, Texas.

Date	Rise	Set
January 16	5:59 p.m.	4:47 a.m.
January 17	5:55 p.m.	4:43 a.m.
January 18	5:51 p.m.	4:40 a.m.
January 19	5:47 p.m.	4:36 a.m.
January 20	5:43 p.m.	4:32 a.m.
January 21	5:39 p.m.	4:28 a.m.
January 22	5:35 p.m.	4:24 a.m.
January 23	5:31 p.m.	4:20 a.m.
January 24	5:27 p.m.	4:16 a.m.
January 25	5:24 p.m.	4:12 a.m.

1. What pattern do you see in rise and set times?

   a. They are getting later every day.   **b.** They are getting earlier every day.

   c. They are staying the same.   **d.** There is no pattern.

2. In which part of the sky will Sirius set on January 21?

   a. east   **b.** west

   c. north   **d.** south

3. Do you think you will always be able to see a star when it rises? Why or why not?

_____

_____

_____

_____

Name: _____ **Date:** _____

Directions: Read the text, and answer the questions.

Laurel is studying ways to see the motion of stars in the sky. She knows that the stars move about 2.5 degrees in 10 minutes. She holds one finger up to the sky and lines Sirius up with the left edge of her index finger. The left edge of her finger is on the western side of the sky. In 10 minutes, she holds her finger up to the sky in the same place.

Developing Questions

1. Where will the star be after 10 minutes?

   a. farther to the left of her finger

   b. to the right of her finger

   c. behind her

   d. gone

2. If she goes out again after an hour, where would the star be?

   a. farther west

   b. farther east

   c. the same place

   d. There is no way of knowing.

3. If Sirius has moved about two finger widths in 10 minutes, about how many degrees does one of her fingers measure? How do you know?

   _____

   _____

   _____

   _____

Name: _____ **Date:** _____

Planning Solutions

Directions: Read the text, and answer the questions.

Laurel wants to try using her camera to track the motion of the stars. One way to see the movement is take a long-exposure photo of the stars. This means you take a photo where the camera's shutter is open for much longer than normal. If you take a photo with a five-minute exposure, you will see the stars as small lines in the sky. Stars move about 2.5 degrees in 10 minutes.

1. How will the photo look different if Laurel does a one-hour exposure?

   a. The lines will be longer.

   b. The lines will be shorter.

   c. The lines will change colors.

   d. The lines will disappear.

2. If Laurel takes a photo with a five-minute exposure, how many degrees will the stars have moved?

   a. 2.5 degrees

   b. 1.25 degrees

   c. 5 degrees

   d. 7.5 degrees

3. What else could you use a long-exposure photo to track in the night sky?

   _____

   _____

   _____

Name: _____ **Date:** _____

Directions: Draw yourself using a method to track the movement of the stars. Label your drawing, and answer the questions.

1. Explain the method that you're using in your picture.

_____

_____

_____

2. Why did you choose this method?

_____

_____

Learning Content

Name: _____ **Date:** _____

Directions: Read the text, and answer the questions.

Seasonal Stars

Earth travels around the sun in about 365 days, which is what we call one year. Although stars are always visible at night, we do not always see the same stars in every season. Certain constellations are only visible in certain seasons. Constellations are patterns of stars that look similar to an animal, person, or pretend creature.

If you watch the sky for long enough at night, you will see that the stars rise and set, just like the sun. Over time, however, all of the stars shift from east to west. Eventually the stars we were looking at disappear out of view completely and are replaced by a new batch. After a year, the whole cycle starts again. This is because of Earth's rotation around the sun. At different times of year, Earth is facing different parts of the sky. We can only see the stars that we are facing at night.

1. How long does it take for the cycle of visible stars to complete?

   a. 1 month   **b.** 1 night

   c. 1 year   **d.** 10 years

2. What causes the visible stars to change throughout the year?

   a. Earth revolving around the sun   **b.** Earth rotating on its axis

   c. the weather   **d.** clouds

3. Can you tell the season by which constellations are visible? Why or why not?

   _____

   _____

   _____

   _____

Name: _____ **Date:** _____

Directions: Read the text, and look at the chart. Then, answer the questions.

If you live in the Northern Hemisphere, you see one set of stars throughout the year. The Southern Hemisphere sees a different set of stars. As Earth travels around the sun, different constellations come into view. Some constellations are visible all year.

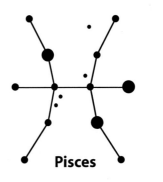
Pisces

Analyzing Data

Season	Constellations Visible in the Northern Hemisphere
winter	Canis Major, Cetus, Eridanus, Gemini, Orion, Perseus, and Taurus
spring	Bootes, Cancer, Crater, Hydra, Leo, and Virgo
summer	Aquila, Cygnus, Hercules, Lyra, Ophiuchus, Sagittarius, and Scorpius
fall	Andromeda, Aquarius, Capricornus, Pegasus, and Pisces
all year	Cassiopeia, Cepheus, Draco, Ursa Major, and Ursa Minor

1. Which constellation can you see all year?

   a. Ursa Major   b. Lyra

   c. Pegasus   d. Gemini

2. In which season are the fewest constellations visible?

   a. winter   b. spring

   c. summer   d. fall

3. When it is winter in the Northern Hemisphere, can you see Orion in the Southern Hemisphere? Why or why not?

   _____

   _____

   _____

Name: _____ **Date:** _____

Directions: Read the text, and answer the questions.

Ronan is looking at the stars one night in January. He sees two bright stars that are next to each other. As he looks longer, he can see the pattern of what looks like two stick figures holding hands. He wants to know more about the constellation.

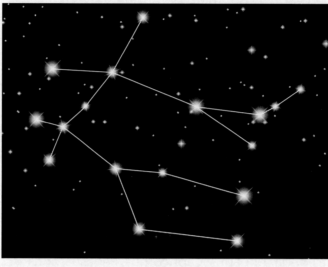

Developing Questions

1. What would be a good resource to help Ronan recognize constellations?

   a. a stargazing book

   b. a website about astronomy

   c. a smartphone app about stars

   d. any of the above

2. Based on the text, what might be the name of this constellation? Might it be Taurus (the Bull) or Gemini (The Twins)? Explain why.

   _____

   _____

   _____

3. What is a question that Ronan could ask about finding other constellations?

   _____

   _____

   _____

51411—180 Days of Science

Name: _____ **Date:** _____

Directions: Read the text, and answer the questions.

Yasmin is camping with her family. Her dad shows her the North Star and explains that it is always in the northern part of Earth's night sky. You can see it from the Northern Hemisphere. It does not rise or set like other stars do. It stays in almost the same spot all night long. You can see the North Star all year long. There are also some constellations near the North Star that you can see in Earth's night sky all year long.

Planning Solutions

1. What could Yasmin use the North Star for while she is camping?

   a. figuring out which direction she is walking during the day

   b. figuring out how to pitch a tent

   c. figuring out which direction she is walking at night

   d. figuring out what constellations are called

2. Is the North Star the only star you can see in Earth's night sky all year long?

   a. Yes, there are no other stars in this part of the night sky.

   b. No, there are some constellations you can see all year.

   c. Yes, even though there constellations, you can't see them.

   d. No, you cannot see the North Star all year long.

3. Does the North Star rise or set the way that other stars do? Why is this important?

   _____

   _____

4. Make a plan for Yasmin to find out more about the North Star.

   _____

   _____

   _____

Name: _____ Date: _____

Communicating Results

Directions: Study the chart. Then, sort the constellations into the correct section of the diagram, and answer the questions.

Constellation	Season Visible in Northern Hemisphere
Scorpius	summer
Orion	winter
Pegasus	fall
Leo	spring
Ursa Minor	all year
Virgo	spring
Taurus	winter
Pisces	fall
Ursa Major	all year
Lyra	summer

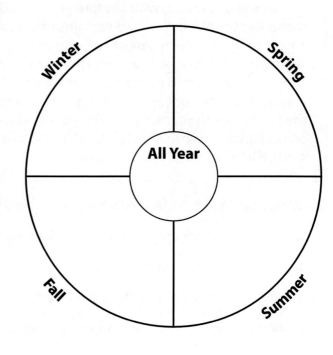

1. Why can't we see Scorpius all year?

   a. Earth rotates around the sun.   **b.** Earth rotates around the moon.

   c. The sun rotates around Earth.   **d.** Earth never faces Scorpius.

2. When can the Northern Hemisphere of Earth see Virgo?

   _____

3. When can the Northern Hemisphere of Earth see Orion?

   _____

4. Explain why we can see some constellations all year.

   _____

   _____

   _____

   _____

Name: _____ Date: _____

Directions: Read the text, and answer the questions.

Tracing Shadows

You can see many patterns in the sky that are signs of Earth's movement through space. You can see signs on the ground, too. Have you ever noticed that shadows change throughout the day? During the early morning or late afternoon, the sun is low in the sky, and shadows are long. When the sun is overhead at noon, shadows are the shortest. The position of a shadow will move throughout the day, just like the position of the sun. You can use the shadows to help tell time.

Learning Content

1. When are shadows shortest?

   a. 10:00 a.m.

   b. 5:00 p.m.

   c. 7:00 a.m.

   d. noon

2. What information can a shadow give you?

   a. rough time of day

   b. your location

   c. weather forecast

   d. season

3. At what rate do shadows move?

   a. the same rate as the sun

   b. faster than the sun

   c. slower than the sun

   d. They don't move.

Analyzing Data

Name: _____ **Date:** _____

Directions: Read the text, and look at the diagram. Then, answer the questions.

> Sundials are the oldest known instruments for telling time. As the sun moves from east to west, the sundial casts a shadow that tells what time it is.

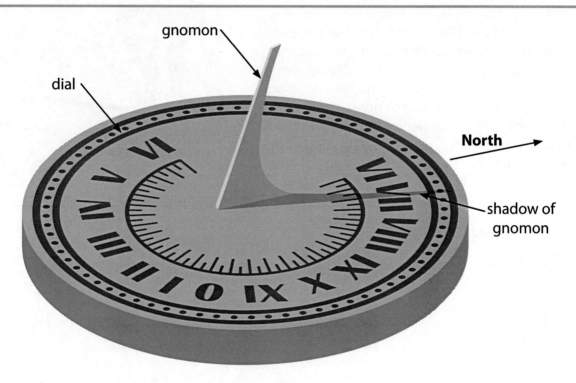

1. What part of the sundial casts the shadow?

   a. dial plate

   b. gnomon

   c. roman numerals

   d. shadow

2. If the sun is in the western part of the sky, which direction will the shadow point?

   a. west

   b. east

   c. north

   d. south

3. The gnomon faces north. Would the sundial work correctly if you pointed the gnomon east? Why or why not?

   _____

   _____

   _____

Developing Questions

Name: _____ **Date:** _____

Directions: Read the text, and answer the questions.

Drew is doing a project to track the movement of shadows. He decides he will go outside and trace his shadow with chalk. He goes out at 10:00 a.m., noon, and 4:00 p.m.

1. What will his shadow be like at 10:00 a.m.?

    a. long and pointed west

    b. long and pointed east

    c. short and pointed west

    d. short and pointed east

2. What will his shadow be like at noon?

    a. very short and close to his body

    b. very long and pointed west

    c. long and pointed west

    d. long and pointed east

3. What is a question that Drew could ask about changes in the position of his shadow?

_____

_____

_____

4. What will his shadow be like at 4:00 p.m.?

_____

_____

Planning Solutions

Name: _____ **Date:** _____

Directions: Read the text, and answer the questions.

Hana is making a simple homemade sundial. She has a paper plate, a pencil, and a printed clock face. She knows that she needs to have the mark for noon pointing north.

1. What will happen to the shadow over the course of the day?

   a. It will gradually move around the clock face.

   b. It will stay in the same place.

   c. It will jump from one side of the clock face to the other.

   d. It will disappear at noon.

2. Will the sundial be accurate at night?

   a. Yes, it will tell time all day.

   b. No, it needs the sun to cast a shadow.

   c. No, it will be off by one hour.

   d. No, it will be off by three hours.

3. Make a plan for Hana to estimate the time of day using shadows if she doesn't have a clock or sundial available.

   _____

   _____

   _____

   _____

   _____

Name: _____ **Date:** _____

Directions: Arthur put a 50 cm stick in the ground and measured the length of the shadow once an hour. Look at the chart, and create a line graph of the data. Then, answer the questions.

Communicating Results

Time	Length of Shadow (cm)
8:00 a.m.	118
9:00 a.m.	82
10:00 a.m.	57
11:00 a.m.	44
12:00 p.m.	35
1:00 p.m.	37

Time	Length of Shadow (cm)
2:00 p.m.	40
3:00 p.m.	47
4:00 p.m.	60
5:00 p.m.	85
6:00 p.m.	120

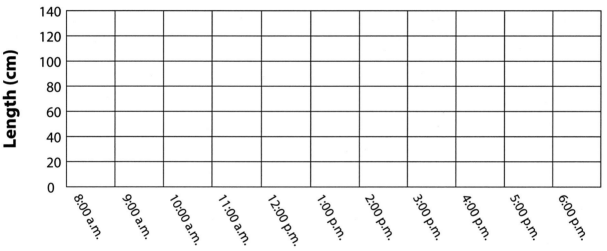

Shadows of 50 cm Stick

1. Describe a pattern you see on the chart.

_____

_____

2. Why does the pattern happen the way it does?

_____

_____

Answer Key

Life Science

Week 1: Day 1 (page 14)
1. b
2. c
3. Possible answer includes, "Because they live different amounts of time and reproduce differently."

Week 1: Day 2 (page 15)
1. c
2. c
3. Possible answer includes, "In stage 2, the frog is tiny and has no legs. In stage 5, It is much larger, has legs, and has a large tail."

Week 1: Day 3 (page 16)
1. b
2. c
3. Possible answer includes, "Which types of insects experience metamorphosis?
4. Answers will vary.

Week 1: Day 4 (page 17)
1. d
2. d
3. Possible answers include, "Ask the farmer," or, "Read a book about farm animals."

Week 1: Day 5 (page 18)

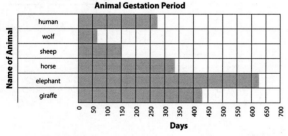

Animal Gestation Period

1. wolf, elephant

Week 2: Day 1 (page 19)
1. c
2. c
3. Possible answer includes, "Middle adulthood and infant/toddler because your body and abilities are completely different in these stages."

Week 2: Day 2 (page 20)
1. d
2. c
3. Possible answer includes, "Walking," or, "Talking."

Week 2: Day 3 (page 21)
1. d
2. b
3. Possible answer includes, "Does everyone go through the stages in the same order?"

Week 2: Day 4 (page 22)
1. d
2. b
3. Possible answer includes, "Observe children of many different ages."

Week 2: Day 5 (page 23)
Grandparent level: late adulthood
Mom/Dad level: middle adulthood
Child level: childhood
1. Answers will vary.
2. Answers will vary.

Week 3: Day 1 (page 24)
1. b
2. d
3. Possible answer includes, "People do not have the hatchling stage," or "People's life cycles have different names."

Week 3: Day 2 (page 25)
1. a
2. a
3. Possible answer includes, "Adult stage because that's when they are fully grown."

Week 3: Day 3 (page 26)
1. c
2. b
3. Possible answer includes, "Why are they going to the ocean?"
4. Possible answer includes, "They grow into adults and later reproduce."

Week 3: Day 4 (page 27)
1. d
2. d
3. Possible answer includes, "Measure it to see how long it is."
4. Possible answer includes: snakes, other lizards, turtles

Answer Key (cont.)

Week 3: Day 5 (page 28)

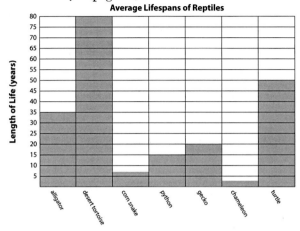

Average Lifespans of Reptiles

Week 4: Day 1 (page 29)
1. c
2. d
3. Possible answers include: dogs, cats, birds, hamsters.

Week 4: Day 2 (page 30)
1. d
2. a
3. Frogs spend time on both land and in water, and cats only live on land.

Week 4: Day 3 (page 31)
1. c
2. d
3. Possible answer includes, "What kind of vertebrae did the skeleton belong to?"

Week 4: Day 4 (page 32)
1. c
2. b
3. Possible answer includes, "She would need to create a flexible backbone and cover it with soft material."

Week 4: Day 5 (page 33)
Lion: vertebrate, terrestrial
Snake: vertebrate, terrestrial
Shark: vertebrate, aquatic
Jellyfish: invertebrate, aquatic
Lizard: vertebrate, terrestrial
Bee: invertebrate, terrestrial
Tick: invertebrate, terrestrial
Tuna: vertebrate, aquatic
Clam: invertebrate: aquatic
Pigeon: vertebrate, terrestrial
Ladybug: invertebrate, terrestrial
Octopus: invertebrate, aquatic

Week 5: Day 1 (page 34)
1. d
2. a
3. a
4. Possible answer includes, "No, because everyone's traits are unique."

Week 5: Day 2 (page 35)
1. c
2. a
3. c

Week 5: Day 3 (page 36)
1. a
2. d
3. Possible answer includes, "Do sisters inherit different traits?"
4. Possible answer includes, "Yes, because they inherited all the same traits."

Week 5: Day 4 (page 37)
1. a
2. a
3. Possible answer includes, "Ask him if either of his parents have blue eyes."
4. Answers will vary.

Week 5: Day 5 (page 38)
Straight hair: inherited
Eye color: inherited
Skin color: inherited
Playing an Instrument: acquired
1. Answers will vary, but may include things like: playing an instrument, riding a bike.
2. Answers will vary, but should include things like: hair color, hair texture, eye color, skin color.

Answer Key *(cont.)*

Week 6: Day 1 (page 39)
1. b
2. a
3. Possible answer includes, "They help animals survive."

Week 6: Day 2 (page 40)
1. d
2. a

Week 6: Day 3 (page 41)
1. b
2. a
3. Possible answer includes, "Why do birds build nests in trees?"
4. Answers will vary.

Week 6: Day 4 (page 42)
1. b
2. a
3. Possible answer includes, "She could teach him by using treats."
4. Possible answers include: how to shake paws, how to heel

Week 6: Day 5 (page 43)
Possible answers for chart:
Cat learned behavior: using a litter box
Cat instinct: being awake at night
Dog learned behavior: playing fetch
Dog instinct: wagging their tail
1. Answers will vary.
2. Possible answer includes, "A learned behavior for a parrot could be saying human words. An instinct would be building a nest."

Week 7: Day 1 (page 44)
1. b
2. c
3. b
4. Possible answer includes, "One example is clover, a rabbit, a fox, and a worm."

Week 7: Day 2 (page 45)
1. a
2. c
3. a

Week 7: Day 3 (page 46)
1. a
2. c
3. Possible answer includes, "Does energy only flow one direction in the food chain?"

Week 7: Day 4 (page 47)
1. c
2. a
3. Possible answer includes, "Observe the animals in the environment and watch what they eat."

Week 7: Day 5 (page 48)
Clover: producer
Rabbit: primary consumer
Fox: secondary consumer
Earthworm: decomposer
1. Possible answer includes, "Humans are at the top of the food chain because we don't have any natural predators."
2. Decomposer

Week 8: Day 1 (page 49)
1. b
2. c
3. a

Week 8: Day 2 (page 50)
1. d
2. b
3. a

Week 8: Day 3 (page 51)
1. c
2. d
3. Possible answer includes, "What would happen if an organism disappeared from the food web?"

Week 8: Day 4 (page 52)
1. a
2. a
3. Possible answer includes, "Find out if any other animals eat it."
4. Possible answer includes, "Yes, because no animals eat humans."

Week 8: Day 5 (page 53)
Answers will vary. Each box should have an appropriate organism for the stage.

Week 9: Day 1 (page 54)
1. a
2. b
3. d

Week 9: Day 2 (page 55)
1. d
2. a
3. a

Answer Key *(cont.)*

Week 9: Day 3 (page 56)
1. b
2. a
3. Possible answer includes, "How long will it take for the lack of air to hurt a plant?"

Week 9: Day 4 (page 57)
1. a
2. a
3. Possible answer includes, "He could give one plant regular water and not water another one."

Week 9: Day 5 (page 58)
Picture should show the sun, a representation of air, and a representation of water. All items should be labeled.

Week 10: Day 1 (page 59)
1. c
2. a
3. d
4. Possible answers include worms, mushrooms, and mold.

Week 10: Day 2 (page 60)
1. a
2. c
3. b

Week 10: Day 3 (page 61)
1. c
2. a
3. Possible answer includes, "What types of decomposers like what types of decaying matter?"

Week 10: Day 4 (page 62)
1. a
2. b
3. Possible answer includes, "Put some worms and vegetable scraps together in a bucket and observe them."

Week 10: Day 5 (page 63)
Drawings should include things like fruit and vegetable scraps, worms, soil, and water.
1. Possible answer includes, "Decomposers break down decaying matter, and they put nutrients back in the soil for plants."

Week 11: Day 1 (page 64)
1. b
2. a
3. d

Week 11: Day 2 (page 65)
1. d
2. a
3. c

Week 11: Day 3 (page 66)
1. a
2. c
3. Possible answer includes, "Why can't a plant make food without sunlight?"

Week 11: Day 4 (page 67)
1. c
2. a
3. Possible answer includes, "He could try covering one of the plants with a bag so that it doesn't get air."

Week 11: Day 5 (page 68)

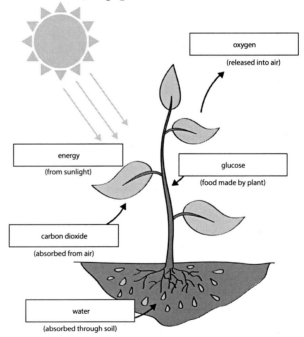

Week 12: Day 1 (page 69)
1. c
2. b
3. Possible answer includes, "They need a stable climate so plants can grow and animals can reproduce."

Week 12: Day 2 (page 70)
1. b
2. d
3. Possible answer includes, "The animals would die because they wouldn't have food."

Answer Key *(cont.)*

Week 12: Day 3 (page 71)
1. d
2. a
3. Possible answer includes, "What all should I add to the ecosystem?"

Week 12: Day 4 (page 72)
1. a
2. Possible answer includes, "Yes, because there wouldn't be enough oxygen for the fish if the plants died."
3. Possible answer includes, "Control the temperature in the tank."

Week 12: Day 5 (page 73)
Students should draw animals that would appear in a pond.
1. Answers will vary.
2. Answers will vary.
3. Possible answers include: pollution, plants dying, animals dying, not enough sun

Physical Science

Week 1: Day 1 (page 74)
1. c
2. b
3. a

Week 1: Day 2 (page 75)
1. b
2. c
3. Possible answer includes, "Yes because it just changed forms."

Week 1: Day 3 (page 76)
1. a
2. a
3. Possible answer includes, "Does the water feel different or smell different?"
4. Possible answer includes, "Yes, because water can only hold a certain amount of salt."

Week 1: Day 4 (page 77)
1. a
2. c
3. Possible answer includes, "Aaron could test different items in fresh water and salt water."
4. Possible answer includes, "The water would evaporate, and the salt would remain."

Week 1: Day 5 (page 78)
1. Possible answer includes, "Add salt."
2. Possible answer includes, "The more salt that is in the water, the more the egg floats."
3. Possible answer includes, "Things float more easily in the ocean."

Week 2: Day 1 (page 79)
1. a
2. c
3. Possible answer includes, "Look at its shape and size."

Week 2: Day 2 (page 80)
1. a
2. d
3. Possible answer includes, "Weigh the balloons."

Week 2: Day 3 (page 81)
1. b
2. b
3. Possible answer includes, "How can I use air in different ways to keep the figurine from moving?"

Week 2: Day 4 (page 82)
1. c
2. a
3. Possible answer includes, "She could wrap three non-fragile items in the three packing materials and see which one seems the most protected."
4. Possible answer includes, "You could use bags filled with air and pack them around the box."

Week 2: Day 5 (page 83)
Answers will vary.

Week 3: Day 1 (page 84)
1. d
2. a
3. Possible answer includes, "Blow on it."

Week 3: Day 2 (page 85)
1. b
2. b
3. Possible answer includes, "You could use a fan because the air will always blow with the same force on the same setting."

Week 3: Day 3 (page 86)
1. b
2. a
3. Possible answer includes, "What is the most important element of the balloon rocket?"

Answer Key *(cont.)*

Week 3: Day 4 (page 87)

1. d
2. a
3. Possible answer includes, "He could place a book on top of the balloon, and then he could inflate the balloon to lift it."

Week 3: Day 5 (page 88)

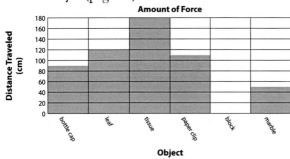

1. Possible answer includes, "The block is too heavy."

Week 4: Day 1 (page 89)

1. a
2. a
3. a
4. Possible answer includes, "Because it dissolves."

Week 4: Day 2 (page 90)

1. d
2. b
3. It will not change.

Week 4: Day 3 (page 91)

1. b
2. a
3. a
4. Possible answer includes, "Does cooking the ingredients affect the weight?"
5. No

Week 4: Day 4 (page 92)

1. b
2. d
3. Possible answer includes, "Weigh the pot before and after cooking."

Week 4: Day 5 (page 93)

Amount of Sugar (cups)	Amount of Water (cups)	Amount of Lemon Juice (cups)	Total Lemonade (cups)
1	4	1	6
2	8	2	12
3	12	3	18
4	16	4	24

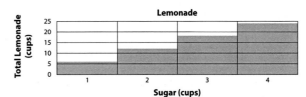

1. Possible answer includes, "Yes, because there will still be the same amount of sugar dissolved in the same amount of liquid."

Week 5: Day 1 (page 94)

1. a
2. c
3. d

Week 5: Day 2 (page 95)

1. a
2. c
3. It will stay the same.

Week 5: Day 3 (page 96)

1. b
2. c
3. Possible answer includes, "How can I tell that the water weighs the same as the ice?"

Week 5: Day 4 (page 97)

1. b
2. a
3. Possible answer includes, "Weigh both coolers before and after the ice melts."

Week 5: Day 5 (page 98)

1. It increases.
2. It stays the same.
3. Possible answer includes, "Some water spilled."
4. Possible answer includes, "The weight would increase."

Week 6: Day 1 (page 99)

1. c
2. b
3. a
4. Possible answer includes, "No, you can examine things like color and mass without changing the object."

Answer Key (cont.)

Week 6: Day 2 (page 100)
1. c
2. a
3. c
4. Possible answer includes, "You should look at the reaction to vinegar."

Week 6: Day 3 (page 101)
1. a
2. d
3. Possible answer includes, "How would they react to water?"
4. Possible answer includes, "No, because they all have different properties."

Week 6: Day 4 (page 102)
1. a
2. c
3. Possible answer includes, "Test each substance with each liquid."
4. Possible answer includes, "No, because he wouldn't know which liquid was causing a reaction."

Week 6: Day 5 (page 103)

	Color	Reaction to Water	Reaction to Vinegar	Reaction to Iodine
Powder A	white	none	bubbled	none
Powder B	white	none	none	blue-black
Powder C	white	none	none	none

1. Possible answer includes, "I think Powder A is baking soda because it bubbled with vinegar. Powder B is cornstarch because it turned blue-black with iodine. Powder C is powdered sugar because it had no reactions."
2. Baking powder
3. Possible answer includes, "Kirk is testing chemical properties. Physical properties are things like color and mass. Chemical properties are how substances react to other substances."

Week 7: Day 1 (page 104)
1. c
2. a
3. b
4. b
5. Possible answer includes, "Forks and knives."

Week 7: Day 2 (page 105)
1. a
2. d
3. c

Week 7: Day 3 (page 106)
1. a
2. a
3. Possible answer includes, "How soft are the different metals?"
4. Possible answer includes, "Foil is flexible, and the pan is not."

Week 7: Day 4 (page 107)
1. c
2. a
3. Possible answer includes, "She could see if magnets stick to any of the metals."
4. Possible answer includes, "Look at the color."

Week 7: Day 5 (page 108)

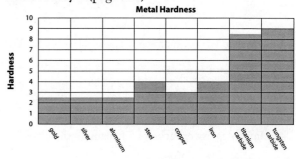

1. Answers could include buildings, jewelry, or kitchen items.

Week 8: Day 1 (page 109)
1. d
2. a
3. b
4. Possible answer includes, "A physical change can often be reversed, and a chemical change usually can't be reversed."

Week 8: Day 2 (page 110)
1. b
2. a
3. c

Week 8: Day 3 (page 111)
1. b
2. b
3. Possible answer includes, "How much should I increase the baking soda in each trial?"
4. Possible answer includes, "Yes, because it will help him make sure he is getting accurate results."

Answer Key *(cont.)*

Week 8: Day 4 (page 112)
1. c
2. b
3. Possible answer includes, "He should complete each trial three times."
4. Possible answer includes, "Take notes about the results of each trial."

Week 8: Day 5 (page 113)

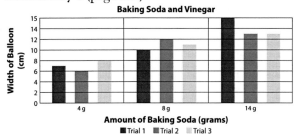

1. 14 grams
2. Possible answer includes, "You could get a larger reaction because there would be more baking soda in the same amount of vinegar."

Week 9: Day 1 (page 114)
1. b
2. a
3. Possible answer includes, "No, because the mixture of ingredients creates a new substance."
4. chemical change

Week 9: Day 2 (page 115)
1. b
2. a
3. Possible answer includes, "Because it results in a new substance."

Week 9: Day 3 (page 116)
1. d
2. b
3. Possible answer includes, "What is happening during the chemical change?"
4. Possible answer includes, "Because a new substance is made."

Week 9: Day 4 (page 117)
1. b
2. c
3. Possible answer includes, "Try different amounts of yeast and do three trials with each different amount."
4. Possible answer includes, "The fluffy bread because it had more gas to make bubbles. The bubbles are what make the bread fluffy, and the yeast makes the bubbles."

Week 9: Day 5 (page 118)
Drawings will vary.
1. Answers will vary.

Week 10: Day 1 (page 119)
1. c
2. a
3. d
4. Possible answer includes, "No, because we cannot make food directly from sunlight."

Week 10: Day 2 (page 120)
1. b
2. c
3. Possible answer includes, "It would gain weight because it would have to store the extra food energy as fat."

Week 10: Day 3 (page 121)
1. c
2. d
3. Possible answer includes, "How much energy is lost when the energy transfers from the grasshoppers to the chickens?"

Week 10: Day 4 (page 122)
1. b
2. c
3. Possible answer includes, "Make a meal that is made of plants."

Week 10: Day 5 (page 123)
Drawings will vary but should show energy from sun transferring to plants and then to humans or to plants, animals, and then humans.
1. Answers will vary but should demonstrate an understanding that energy transfers from the sun to producers and from producers to consumers.

Week 11: Day 1 (page 124)
1. b
2. c
3. Possible answer includes, "Plants and animals."
4. Possible answer includes, "Because of things like digesting food to use for energy."

Week 11: Day 2 (page 125)
1. b
2. c
3. Possible answer includes, "No, because secondary consumers eat other animals."

Answer Key *(cont.)*

Week 11: Day 3 (page 126)

1. c
2. b
3. Possible answer includes, "Why is so much energy lost in the transfer?"

Week 11: Day 4 (page 127)

1. c
2. a
3. Possible answer includes, "Matt can research how much energy is in different kinds of food."

Week 11: Day 5 (page 128)

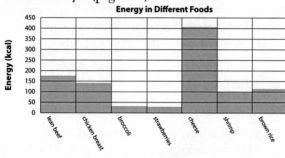

1. Cheese has the most energy. Strawberries have the least.

Week 12: Day 1 (page 129)

1. c
2. b
3. No
4. Possible answer includes, "Because gravity pulls everything toward the center of Earth."

Week 12: Day 2 (page 130)

1. b
2. a
3. b

Week 12: Day 3 (page 131)

1. Possible answer includes, "Because the gravity is lower on the moon than it is on Earth."
2. b
3. Possible answer includes, "How much gravity would it take to keep me from jumping?"

Week 12: Day 4 (page 132)

1. a
2. a
3. Possible answer includes, "He could test different objects with different weights. He should repeat each trial three times."

Week 12: Day 5 (page 133)

Location	Mass (kg)	Gravity	Weight (kg)
Earth	35	1	35
outer space	35	0	0
Earth's moon	35	0.17	5.95
Venus	35	0.90	31.5
Mars	35	0.38	13.3
Mercury	35	0.38	13.3
Jupiter	35	2.36	82.6
Saturn	35	0.92	32.2
Uranus	35	0.89	31.15
Neptune	35	1.13	39.55

1. Jupiter
2. Jupiter
3. Outer space
4. Earth's moon because gravity is the least.

Earth and Space Science

Week 1: Day 1 (page 134)

1. b
2. d
3. a

Week 1: Day 2 (page 135)

1. a
2. b
3. b

Week 1: Day 3 (page 136)

1. a
2. a
3. a
4. Possible answer includes, "How does the oxygen from marine plants end up in the air?"

Week 1: Day 4 (page 137)

1. d
2. c
3. Possible answer includes, "He could draw the different zones of the oceans and the types of creatures that live in each."

Week 1: Day 5 (page 138)

euphotic zone: bright sunlight, lots of animals, warmest water
disphotic zone: dim light, few animals, colder water
aphotic zone: no sunlight, very few animals, coldest water

1. Possible answer includes, "There is no sunlight, and it is extremely cold."

Answer Key *(cont.)*

Week 2: Day 1 (page 139)
1. b
2. a
3. Possible answer includes, "They cause the air to rise, cool, and condense."

Week 2: Day 2 (page 140)
1. a
2. b
3. Possible answer includes, "There are more plants because there is more rain."
4. Possible answer includes, "Yes, because there would be different food sources available."

Week 2: Day 3 (page 141)
1. a
2. a
3. Possible answer includes, "What types of animals live in the different climates?"

Week 2: Day 4 (page 142)
1. b
2. a
3. Possible answer includes, "She could build a mountain with clay and paint one side green and the other side brown."

Week 2: Day 5 (page 143)
Answers will vary. Drawings should demonstrate knowledge of how wind causes clouds to form on the windward side of mountains. Plants should be represented on windward side. Leeward side should be drier.

Week 3: Day 1 (page 144)
1. a
2. b
3. rivers and lakes
4. Possible answer includes, "Because water is a finite resource."

Week 3: Day 2 (page 145)
1. c
2. a
3. d
4. 0.9%
5. Possible answer includes, "No, because it is too hard to access."

Week 3: Day 3 (page 146)
1. a
2. a
3. Possible answer includes, "How much water should I use to represent the water in rivers and lakes?"

Week 3: Day 4 (page 147)
1. b
2. a
3. Possible answer includes, "She could draw a graph."

Week 3: Day 5 (page 148)

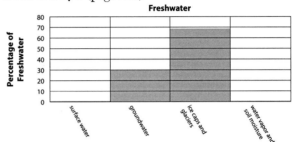

1. Possible answer includes, "Because we don't have a lot of freshwater available."
2. Possible answer includes, "It is frozen. This is important because we can't use it."

Week 4: Day 1 (page 149)
1. a
2. b
3. Possible answer includes, "No, because it would be too hard to get."

Week 4: Day 2 (page 150)
1. b
2. a
3. a
4. Possible answer includes, "Yes, because more ice will stay frozen if it is colder."

Week 4: Day 3 (page 151)
1. a
2. c
3. Possible answer includes, "How much ice should she add to the tray?"
4. Possible answer includes, "She can learn how melting ice can affect coastlines."

Week 4: Day 4 (page 152)
1. d
2. d
3. Possible answer includes, "Add representations of plants and animals to her model."

Answer Key *(cont.)*

Week 4: Day 5 (page 153)

1. Possible answer includes, "It would make it harder for them to find food."
2. Possible answer includes, "It could cause sea levels to rise and beaches to disappear."
3. Possible answer includes, "No because they have been steadily rising."

Week 5: Day 1 (page 154)

1. b
2. a
3. d
4. Possible answer includes, "Some farmers rotate crops and prevent erosion."

Week 5: Day 2 (page 155)

1. b
2. c
3. a
4. applying integrated pest management

Week 5: Day 3 (page 156)

1. a
2. b
3. Possible answer includes, "Why is it better for the livestock to have shelter from trees?"

Week 5: Day 4 (page 157)

1. a
2. b
3. Possible answer includes, "She can ride her bike and take the bus."
4. Possible answer includes, "To make sure cars aren't polluting the air too much."

Week 5: Day 5 (page 158)

Helpful	Harmful
crop rotation	chemical pesticide use
planting cover crops	soil erosion
reducing tillage	wasting water
Clean Air Act of 1970	climate change
	habitat loss

1. Possible answer includes, "It helps keep our air clean."
2. Possible answer includes, "Animals may die because they have no place to live."

Week 6: Day 1 (page 159)

1. d
2. a
3. d
4. Possible answers include: sewage, fertilizer runoff, heat released into water, oil spills

Week 6: Day 2 (page 160)

1. b
2. d
3. a
4. Possible answer includes, "Oil spills because it coats animals in oil."

Week 6: Day 3 (page 161)

1. b
2. d
3. Possible answer includes, "What could I change in my life to help protect water?"
4. Possible answer includes, "Plants and animals could die."

Week 6: Day 4 (page 162)

1. c
2. a
3. Possible answer includes, "Because it could pollute the water."
4. Possible answer includes, "She can pull weeds for her parents so they don't use weed killer."

Week 6: Day 5 (page 163)

Answers will vary.

Week 7: Day 1 (page 164)

1. b
2. a
3. c

Week 7: Day 2 (page 165)

1. d
2. c
3. Possible answer includes: "It is winter when we are tilted away from the sun."

Week 7: Day 3 (page 166)

1. b
2. a
3. Possible answer includes, "What keeps the Earth traveling around the sun?"
4. Possible answer includes, "You could use a large ball to represent the sun and a small ball to represent Earth. Someone could hold the "sun," and the other person could walk "Earth" around them."

Week 7: Day 4 (page 167)

1. a
2. a
3. Possible answer includes, "He could hold a small ball and spin in circles as he walks around the sun."

Answer Key *(cont.)*

Week 7: Day 5 (page 168)

Drawings should include the sun and the Earth's orbit around it. The Earth should have a tilted axis and a moon.

1. Possible answer includes, "The tilt causes the seasons."

Week 8: Day 1 (page 169)

1. c
2. a
3. c
4. Possible answer includes, "We need time zones to standardize time."

Week 8: Day 2 (page 170)

1. a
2. a
3. Possible answer includes, "The Earth spinning on its axis."

Week 8: Day 3 (page 171)

1. b
2. a
3. Possible answer includes, "How long does the moon take to revolve around Earth?"
4. Possible answer includes, "It would help them see how the sun shines on Earth."

Week 8: Day 4 (page 172)

1. a
2. a
3. Possible answer includes, "Riku could call when it is 7:00 p.m. his time. This would be 9:00 a.m. the next day in Tokyo."
4. Possible answer includes, "Yes, because it would be hard to adjust to the new time."

Week 8: Day 5 (page 173)

Drawings will vary.

1. We have day and night because the Earth spins on its axis.

Week 9: Day 1 (page 174)

1. c
2. c
3. Possible answer includes, "No, there are much larger stars. It just looks the biggest from Earth because it is the closest."
4. Possible answer includes, "No, they are not the same. Closer stars look brighter even if they are not actually brighter."

Week 9: Day 2 (page 175)

1. c
2. Possible answer includes, "No, because it is fainter than what our eyes can see."
3. Possible answer includes, "Yes because outer space is limitless."

Week 9: Day 3 (page 176)

1. b
2. a
3. Possible answer includes, "How do you use Orion's belt to find it?"

Week 9: Day 4 (page 177)

1. b
2. c
3. Possible answer includes, "He should look up which constellation is attached to the North Star and what it looks like."

Week 9: Day 5 (page 178)

Graphs will vary. There should be mostly faint stars. There should be few bright stars.

Week 10: Day 1 (page 179)

1. a
2. c
3. c

Week 10: Day 2 (page 180)

1. b
2. b
3. Possible answer includes, "No, because it might be too bright outside."

Week 10: Day 3 (page 181)

1. b
2. a
3. Possible answer includes, "About 1 degree because a star moves 2.5 degrees in 10 minutes."

Week 10: Day 4 (page 182)

1. a
2. b
3. Possible answer includes, "You could track the motion of the moon."

Week 10: Day 5 (page 183)

Drawings and answers will vary.

Week 11: Day 1 (page 184)

1. c
2. a
3. Possible answer includes, "Yes, because only certain constellations are visible every season."

Answer Key (cont.)

Week 11: Day 2 (page 185)
1. a
2. d
3. Possible answer includes, "No, because winter is when you can see Orion from the Northern Hemisphere."

Week 11: Day 3 (page 186)
1. d
2. Possible answer includes, "Gemini the twins because it looks like two stick figures."
3. Possible answer includes "How can I find out what other constellations look like?"

Week 11: Day 4 (page 187)
1. c
2. b
3. Possible answer includes, "No, it does not rise and set the same way because it is always visible at night, and it doesn't look like it moves."
4. Possible answer includes, "She can research the North Star in an encyclopedia."

Week 11: Day 5 (page 188)

1. a
2. Spring
3. Winter
4. Because the Northern Hemisphere is always facing these constellations.

Week 12: Day 1 (page 189)
1. d
2. a
3. a

Week 12: Day 2 (page 190)
1. b
2. b
3. Possible answer includes, "No, because it would cast the shadow in the wrong place on the dial."

Week 12: Day 3 (page 191)
1. a
2. a
3. Possible answer includes, "Will my shadow always move at the same rate as the sun?"
4. long and pointed east

Week 12: Day 4 (page 192)
1. a
2. b
3. Possible answer includes, "She could look at the shadows of a tree to estimate the time of day."

Week 12: Day 5 (page 193)

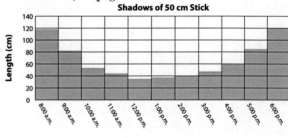

1. Possible answer includes, "The shadow starts out long, gets shorter, and then gets longer again."
2. Possible answer includes, "Because of the motion of the sun across the sky."

Plant Diagram

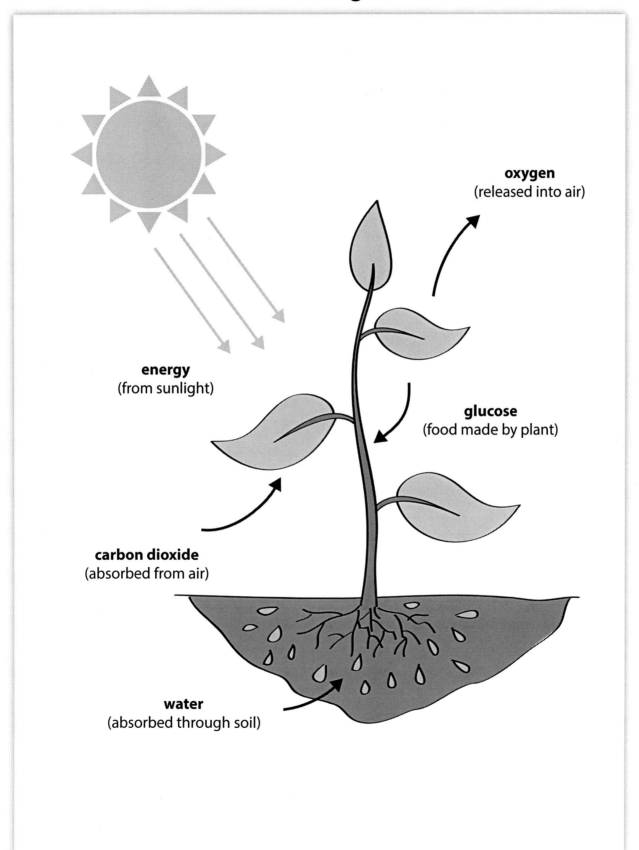

oxygen
(released into air)

energy
(from sunlight)

glucose
(food made by plant)

carbon dioxide
(absorbed from air)

water
(absorbed through soil)

Rain Shadow Diagram

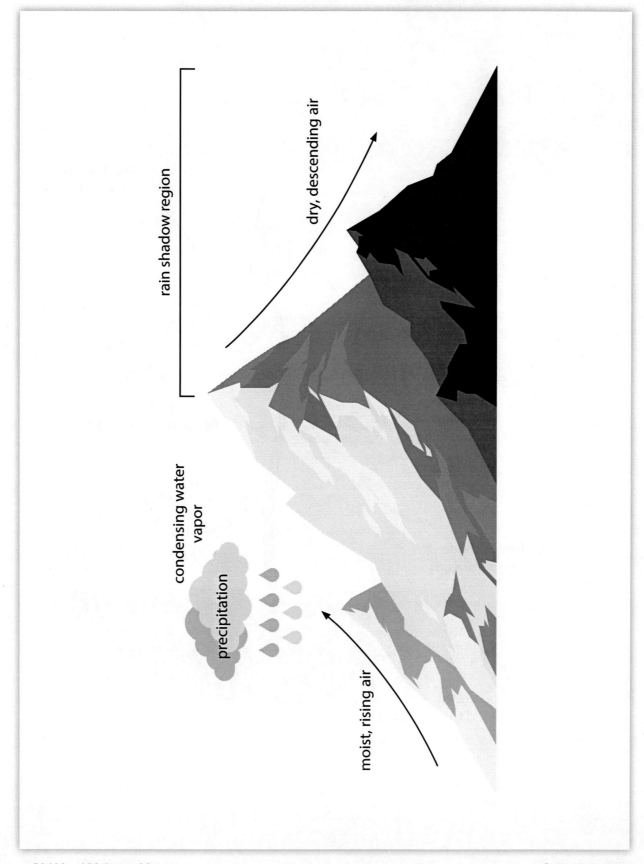

Notes

_____

_____

_____

_____

_____

_____

_____

_____

_____

_____

_____

_____

_____

_____

_____

_____

_____

_____

_____

_____

_____

_____

Student Name: _____ Date: _____

Developing Questions Rubric

Directions: Complete this rubric every four weeks to evaluate students' Day 3 activity sheets. Only one rubric is needed per student. Their work over the four weeks can be evaluated together. Evaluate their work in each category by writing a score in each row. Then, add up their scores, and write the total on the line. Students may earn up to 5 points in each row and up to 15 points total.

Skill	5	3	1	Score
Forming Scientific Inquiries	Forms scientific inquiries related to text all or nearly all the time.	Forms scientific inquiries related to text most of the time.	Does not form scientific inquiries related to text.	
Interpreting Text	Correctly interprets texts to answer questions all or nearly all the time.	Correctly interprets texts to answer questions most of the time.	Does not correctly interpret texts to answer questions.	
Applying Information	Applies new information to form scientific questions all or nearly all the time.	Applies new information to form scientific questions most of the time.	Does not apply new information to form scientific questions.	

Total Points: _____

Student Name: _____ Date: _____

Planning Solutions Rubric

Directions: Complete this rubric every four weeks to evaluate students' Day 4 activity sheets. Only one rubric is needed per student. Their work over the four weeks can be evaluated together. Evaluate their work in each category by writing a score in each row. Then, add up their scores, and write the total on the line. Students may earn up to 5 points in each row and up to 15 points total.

Skill	5	3	1	Score
Planning Investigations	Plans reasonable investigations to study topics all or nearly all the time.	Plans reasonable investigations to study topics most of the time.	Does not plan reasonable investigations to study topics.	
Making Predictions	Studies events to make reasonable predictions all or nearly all the time.	Studies events to make reasonable predictions most of the time.	Does not study events to make reasonable predictions.	
Choosing Next Steps	Chooses reasonable next steps for investigations all or nearly all the time.	Chooses reasonable next steps for investigations most of the time.	Does not choose reasonable next steps for investigations.	

Total Points: _____

Student Name: _____ Date: _____

Communicating Results Rubric

Directions: Complete this rubric every four weeks to evaluate students' Day 5 activity sheets. Only one rubric is needed per student. Their work over the four weeks can be evaluated together. Evaluate their work in each category by writing a score in each row. Then, add up their scores, and write the total on the line. Students may earn up to 5 points in each row and up to 15 points total.

Skill	5	3	1	Score
Representing Data	Correctly represents data with charts and graphs all or nearly all the time.	Correctly represents data with charts and graphs most of the time.	Does not correctly represents data with charts and graphs.	
Making Connections	Makes reasonable connections between new information and prior knowledge all or nearly all the time.	Makes reasonable connections between new information and prior knowledge most of the time.	Does not make reasonable connections between new information and prior knowledge.	
Explaining Results	Uses evidence to accurately explain results all or nearly all the time.	Uses evidence to accurately explain results most of the time.	Does not use evidence to accurately explain results.	

Total Points: _____

Life Science Analysis Chart

Directions: Record the total of each student's Day 1 and Day 2 scores from the four weeks. Then, record each student's rubric scores (pages 210–212). Add the totals, and record the sums in the Total Scores column. Record the average class score in the last row.

Student Name	Week 4						Week 8						Week 12						Total Scores
	Day 1	Day 2	DQ	PS	CR		Day 1	Day 2	DQ	PS	CR		Day 1	Day 2	DQ	PS	CR		
Average Classroom Score																			

DQ = Developing Questions, PS = Planning Solutions, CR = Communicating Results

Physical Science Analysis Chart

Directions: Record the total of each student's Day 1 and Day 2 scores from the four weeks. Then, record each student's rubric scores (pages 210–212). Add the totals, and record the sums in the Total Scores column. Record the average class score in the last row.

Student Name	Week 4						Week 8						Week 12						Total Scores
	Day 1	Day 2	DQ	PS	CR		Day 1	Day 2	DQ	PS	CR		Day 1	Day 2	DQ	PS	CR		
Average Classroom Score																			

DQ = Developing Questions, PS = Planning Solutions, CR = Communicating Results

Earth and Space Science Analysis Chart

Directions: Record the total of each student's Day 1 and Day 2 scores from the four weeks. Then, record each student's rubric scores (pages 210–212). Add the totals, and record the sums in the Total Scores column. Record the average class score in the last row.

Student Name	Week 4 Day 1	Day 2	DQ	PS	CR	Week 8 Day 1	Day 2	DQ	PS	CR	Week 12 Day 1	Day 2	DQ	PS	CR	Total Scores
Average Classroom Score																

DQ = Developing Questions, PS = Planning Solutions, CR = Communicating Results

Digital Resources

To access digital resources, go to this website and enter the following code: 72530049
www.teachercreatedmaterials.com/administrators/download-files/

Rubrics

Resource	Filename
Developing Questions Rubric	questionsrubric.pdf
Planning Solutions Rubric	solutionsrubric.pdf
Communicating Results Rubric	resultsrubric.pdf

Item Analysis Sheets

Resource	Filename
Life Science Analysis Chart	LSanalysischart.pdf
	LSanalysischart.docx
	LSanalysischart.xlsx
Physical Science Analysis Chart	PSanalysischart.pdf
	PSanalysischart.docx
	PSanalysischart.xlsx
Earth and Space Science Analysis Chart	ESSanalysischart.pdf
	ESSanalysischart.docx
	ESSanalysischart.xlsx

Standards

Resource	Filename
Standards Charts	standards.pdf